CHASING
THE
IMPOSSIBLE

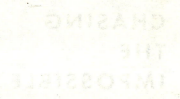

RACHELLE
RUTHERFORD

CHASING THE IMPOSSIBLE

A MODEL FOR INCLUSIVE AND INNOVATIVE CARE

Forbes | Books

Published by Forbes Books, Charleston, South Carolina.
An imprint of Advantage Media Group.

Forbes Books is a registered trademark, and the Forbes Books colophon is a trademark of Forbes Media, LLC.

Printed in the United States of America.

10 9 8 7 6 5 4 3 2

ISBN: 979-8-88750-411-7 (Hardcover)
ISBN: 979-8-88750-636-4 (Paperback)
ISBN: 979-8-88750-412-4 (eBook)

Library of Congress Control Number: 2024910540

Cover design by Lance Buckley.
Layout design by Matthew Morse.

This custom publication is intended to provide accurate information and the opinions of the author in regard to the subject matter covered. It is sold with the understanding that the publisher, Forbes Books, is not engaged in rendering legal, financial, or professional services of any kind. If legal advice or other expert assistance is required, the reader is advised to seek the services of a competent professional.

Since 1917, Forbes has remained steadfast in its mission to serve as the defining voice of entrepreneurial capitalism. Forbes Books, launched in 2016 through a partnership with Advantage Media, furthers that aim by helping business and thought leaders bring their stories, passion, and knowledge to the forefront in custom books. Opinions expressed by Forbes Books authors are their own. To be considered for publication, please visit **books.Forbes.com**.

TO MY CREATOR, MY GOD. You directed and guided me through this process. You trusted me and created the opportunity for the voices of these families to be heard. I am grateful for your goodness and grace.

TO MY HUSBAND, SCOTT. You are my rock, my champion, and the keeper of my heart. Everything that I am would not exist without you.

TO MY CHILDREN, GRANT, EVAN, GRACE, EVA, AUBRI, AND GABE. You are my heart and my greatest legacy. My love for you knows no bounds. Remember, there is no such thing as impossible; answer the call, jump in with both feet, and expect miracles.

TO KAREN HAHNE AND BRENDA WINEGAR. You represent a mother's endless love for her children. Your compassion to reach beyond your own family to help other children and families is the purest form of charity. Your courage and contributions to children and families has left a legacy of love. You inspire all of us to chase the impossible.

TO REED HAHNE AND BECCA WINEGAR. Thank you for your fortitude and leadership and for being a beacon of light and hope for all of us.

TO ALL THE FAMILIES who contributed their stories to this book. You are the heart and soul of this book. May your voices always resonate and pierce the hearts of those who hear your words.

Rachelle Rutherford's *Chasing the Impossible* is a powerful call to action, woven with heart-stirring narratives that ignite the spirit of altruism and innovation. It brilliantly showcases the journey of entrepreneurs, parents, and a community rallying together to transcend the bounds of what seemed unattainable. Through stories of tenacity in the face of adversity, Rutherford invites us all to contribute our unique talents toward building a brighter future for children with disabilities. This book is not just a testament to human resilience but also a roadmap for mobilizing support and resources on a scale previously deemed impossible. As someone deeply committed to making a difference, I found *Chasing the Impossible* to be a compelling reminder that our collective efforts can transform lives and reshape futures. Rachelle Rutherford's work is an essential read for anyone looking to leave a mark on the world by challenging the status quo and pursuing the impossible.

—CHAD HYMAS

Best-Selling Author and Hall of Fame Speaker

In a system littered with shortcomings and obstacles, Rachelle boldly brings forth solutions and energy for change. *Chasing the Impossible* addresses two of the most important factors in the disability landscape right now, the stories of those being impacted and solutions. There is a power in the story that stems from the introduction, where even the author had to explore her own role in helping. *Chasing the Impossible* provides a framework and motivation for the role that we each have in making the world a better place.

—DEREK J. LEE, PHD, CRC, LPCC-S, DBTC, CAMSC
CEO, The Hope Institute & Perrysburg Counseling Services;
Professor, Texas Tech University Health Science Center

Rachelle's *Chasing the Impossible* is a masterpiece that captivates and motivates you to dig deeper into giving more of yourself than you thought possible. She touches and inspires your soul, compelling you to serve others more effectively and sincerely from the heart. Her storytelling and personal experiences touched my heart, leaving an unforgettable mark for those who feel called to make a difference and those who want to leave a lasting legacy of meaningful service and contribution. Rachelle is a game-changer and a beacon of hope for children with special needs as well as for those who desire to live their highest purpose and calling.

—SETEMA GALI
Coach and Keynote Speaker

Rachelle has done a fantastic job of presenting the moving history and exciting future of Kids on the Move in *Chasing the Impossible.* She and her management team left successful corporate positions to make a difference for future generations, one child at a time, and their impact is being felt by the children, their families, and the community. I hope that more individuals and businesses will support KOTM by contributing time, money, and resources to this important cause.

—EDGIE E. DONAKEY
Technology Executive, Mentor, and former Chairman, KOTM

Chasing the Impossible is an amazing representation of the life-changing services that programs such as KOTM provide to families. There is a passion that is ignited in the individuals who serve children with disabilities and their families. That passion often is what fuels innovation in services provided and the funding to support the needed services. This book highlights how people without any previous connection to those who have disabilities can make a life-changing impact on the community and the families that they serve.

—JULIA HOOD, PHD, BCBA-D, NCSP
Assistant Professor, University of Utah

When it comes to parenting kids with superpowers—unique gifts, special abilities that come coupled with exceptional needs and neurodivergence—there's a great many places we can go to be filled with despair. The people behind this book and their story offer a refreshing well of hope from which all of us can drink deeply.

—STEVEN SHARP NELSON
Composer, speaker, and cellist of "The Piano Guys"

Indeed, a diagnosis of one disability or another may define the obstacles or challenges a child faces, but it does not define who the child is. Each child will have their own preferences, areas of interest, and distinct personality. All of us know families that face the unexpected challenges of raising a child with a disability. *Chasing the Impossible* is compassionate, faith promoting, and inspirational for all who love children and have a desire to help them reach up and become all that they can become.

—TOM SMITH
New York Times Best-Selling Author, *The Oz Principle*

CONTENTS

ACKNOWLEDGMENTS...................................1

INTRODUCTION
A CALL TO ACTION............................. 5

CHAPTER 1
ONE CHILD AT A TIME 11

CHAPTER 2
FINDING HOPE 35

CHAPTER 3
CARE 55

CHAPTER 4
UNWAVERING INTEGRITY 73

CHAPTER 5
EXPERT CARE FOR LONG-TERM SUCCESS.......... 93

CHAPTER 6
LIGHTENING THE LOAD 117

CHAPTER 7
INCLUSION IS FOR EVERYONE. 141

CHAPTER 8
NO SUCH THING AS IMPOSSIBLE 159

ABOUT THE AUTHOR. 181

CONTACT 183

ACKNOWLEDGMENTS

I want to acknowledge and thank those individuals and groups who have helped me become the person I am today, for inspiring me and believing in me. This book was possible because of you and your tremendous support, help, and encouragement.

It is a privilege and honor to give a voice to children and families. Chasing the impossible takes courage—it's a decision to move beyond what is comfortable. To lean into the darkness. To reach outside of yourself for something greater. To lift and elevate another. To love deeper. To connect further. To rise higher and leave a triumphant legacy of heroic and historic measure.

The Hahne and Winegar Families: To Karen Hahne, Bob Hahne, Reed Hahne, and the rest of the Hahne family. To Brenda Winegar, Jim Winegar, Becca Winegar, and the rest of the Winegar family. Back in the 1980s when you set out to change the future for your children with Down syndrome, when society had very few resources available, you provided a safe haven for parents and families so they too could have a bright future. Your legacy empowers parents and grants access to a world of growth and endless possibilities for children with disabilities. Kids on the Move is a testament to your courage, dedication, and love.

The Parents and Caregivers: To all the parents, caregivers, and families supporting a child or loved one with a disability, you chase and conquer the impossible every single day. Thank you for being a beacon of light for all of us. I hope that this book inspires you and gives you hope and strength to reach beyond what you think is possible for your child. I hope you have peace and comfort in knowing you are enough. You are not alone—you have a community behind you, supporting you, and lifting you. It's okay to ask for help and take a much-needed break to refresh, rejuvenate, and recharge. We know there are gaps in support and services in every community, and we are committed to finding solutions and shouldering this responsibility together.

The Children: You bring so much joy and love into every space you enter. You radiate sunshine and bring out the best in people. We slow down and become more mindful, grateful, compassionate, patient, and loving because of you. You are resilient and strong. Keep reaching for the stars! You are a gift to the world, our greatest treasure.

The Families Referenced in This Book: Thank you for your courage and willingness to share your stories, victories, and challenges with the world. They are profound and truly inspirational. The love and commitment to your children is powerful—it has no limits. You inspire all of us to strive to be better parents.

The Kids on the Move Staff: To the compassionate, loving, and dedicated staff at Kids on the Move, thank you for being uniquely you! You are the heart of KOTM! You transform the lives of children and families every single day. Your expertise and quality of care is of the highest caliber. Yet, what sets you apart is your light and love for children and families.

The Kids on the Move Board Of Directors: Thank you for your support and encouragement to capture the story of our founders and the impact KOTM has had on our community during the last forty years. As we look to the future, I am grateful for your endless support of our strategic initiatives and my vision of inclusive and innovative care.

The Forbes Books Team: Thank you so much for your help, guidance, and expertise. I am grateful to each of you on the team and for your unwavering support of my story and the story of Kids on the Move. I am excited for the future books we will publish together.

A CALL TO ACTION

It was just another Tuesday when my phone vibrated across my desk. A familiar name, a colleague of mine, whom we'll call "Mike," flashed across my screen, and I swiped the smooth glass to connect the call, "Well, hello there!" I greeted him as I wondered what the unexpected call was about. We exchanged a few pleasantries before he went on to ask if I would be interested in volunteering as a board member.

For the previous two years, Mike had served on the board of a non-profit local to our community here in Utah, Kids on the Move (KOTM). While I had heard the non-profit's name in passing and knew they worked with children with disabilities, I didn't know much else about the organization. Mike explained that several seats had opened up on the board of directors and that he believed I would be a great fit.

While I was flattered that he would think of me, I wasn't sure if I could be of any real help to the organization. At the time, I was engrossed in running my own company and working for a genealogy non-profit, FamilySearch.org. Not to mention that I am also a busy mom of six children, none of whom has special needs. KOTM was not even on my radar. Honestly, like many families in our country without a close connection to someone with a disability, I knew even less about autism spectrum disorder (ASD), Down syndrome, hydrocephaly, juvenile depression, and any of the dozens of diagnoses that one in six children and their families in the United States face daily.[1]

Sure, I understood that these families have special needs and different education requirements, etc. However, I was blissfully unfamiliar with the challenges that many families with a child with a disability face daily in order to meet their child's basic needs, not to mention securing necessary interventions and therapies.

No, all of that would come later.

On that seemingly mundane Tuesday afternoon, I was just like any other parent of typically developing children. I had my family, and I had my career. My work outside the home focused on helping companies with efficiency, optimization, and long-term sustainability. What could I possibly offer a non-profit organization, which, I'm sure, was absolutely doing good work but whose services had nothing to do with me on a personal or professional level?

Despite my lack of experience or education about KOTM and the people they help, I decided to accept Mike's invitation to sit in on a board meeting, partially as a favor to Mike but also because I strongly believe that you should never turn down the chance to connect with new people. The following week, as I sat in that board room during that two-hour meeting, I felt something shift inside of me. As the

---

1   Centers for Disease Control and Prevention, "CDC's work on developmental disabilities," CDC, May 16, 2022, accessed December 4, 2023, https://www.cdc.gov/ncbddd/developmentaldisabilities/about.html.

board addressed various items and questions on their agenda, I heard story after story of families whose lives were completely changed by this organization.

I walked into that meeting believing that KOTM was simply a place where families could access therapies for their kids. But I walked out, understanding that KOTM was a lifeline to thousands of members of our community. It is a cadre of mothers, fathers, social workers, teachers, leaders, volunteers, doctors, entrepreneurs, attorneys, financial advisors, investors, and more who believe that every child deserves a bright future and volunteer their time and financial resources to help.

After one board meeting, I knew I needed to be a part of this team, but I didn't necessarily know how to contribute. Instead of thinking I had nothing to offer, I started asking, "What can I give that will make a difference?"

That day, something came alive inside of me. While I have always wanted my life to have meaning and to count, I've gone about doing that in the ways that most of us are told to contribute to society.

- Find a career, build a business you love, and do good work. Check.
- Raise a family and love your spouse to the best of your ability. Check.
- Volunteer, and give back to the community in your spare time. Check.

Encountering KOTM made me realize that we are all called to do more than simply check the boxes. Each and every one of us is called to serve the members of our community with our unique gifts and talents.

I hope that within this book, we can paint a picture of the phenomenal families, wonderful staff, and critical services we offer families. But more so, my desire is for you to catch the fire that burns within every parent, staff, and volunteer who has been a part of KOTM—a fire that believes in the potential of every child and in the power of people who use their gift to benefit others. Whether you're a professional, a neighbor, or a friend, your unique skills, time, kindness, and resources can make a difference, specifically for children with disabilities, whom are among our most vulnerable, and most deserving of our unwavering support.

Uncover the Passion Behind the Pages: Discover the Powerful "Why?" Behind My Writing and How These Stories Can Reshape Your Perspective.

chasingtheimpossiblebook.com/why

As we paint this picture, we are painstakingly aware of the incredible power of words. The words that our society has used in the past to describe a disability or someone with a disability have been incredibly harmful. Thankfully, as our understanding has grown and evolved, so have the words we use to describe someone who was born with a condition or disability or who has developed one later in life.

While many of us know that certain words are rude, crass, or downright cruel, it's important to note that how someone wants to describe their diagnosis or disability is often nuanced and incredibly personal. For example, someone may prefer to be described as handiabled as opposed to handicapped. Someone diagnosed with

ASD may prefer to say they have autism, while others like to be described as autistic.

During the course of the book, you will see that I consistently refer to various diagnoses as a *disability* and those who have been diagnosed as someone *with a disability*. When referencing children who do not have a disability, I will do so as *typical* or *typically developing*. The team behind the book and I landed on this terminology for several reasons and believe it warrants an explanation of the use of two very broad terms to address a very nuanced subject.

The words *disability* and *typical* are very common terminology and tend to be universally understood by various communities from a multitude of backgrounds, ethnicities, and experiences. While we love some of the newer terms, such as "all abilities" or "different abilities," we do not want anyone, especially those who are unfamiliar with these different conditions we reference in the book, to misinterpret our meaning.

It is not our heart or intention to mislabel or put any one person into a box they do not fit into but simply to streamline communication in order to better serve the stories of each family. If you meet someone or currently have a relationship with someone who has a disability, we encourage you to open a conversation and ask them about their preferred way of addressing their condition. We want to be as empowering as possible, and what one family considers empowering can be very different from another.

We also want to acknowledge and call out that a child is never their diagnosis. Yes, a diagnosis may define the obstacles or challenges they face, but it does not define who they are. A child with a disability, just like a typically developing child, will have their own preferences, areas of interest, and distinct personality.

As we share these family's stories, you will learn the obstacles they overcame, even when "experts" told them it was impossible. More importantly, you'll come to understand how their lives were transformed and the profound impact KOTM has on our community as a whole. But the last thing I want you to walk away with is stories alone. I want these stories and our passion to move you to action.

We are all capable of more—more kindness, more compassion, and more positive change. Whether it's volunteering, donating financially, or spreading awareness, your contribution matters. As we turn these pages, let the stories, the passion, and the dedication of KOTM inspire you to make a difference. To say yes to that pull on the inside of you to serve something bigger than yourself, and to challenge what was once labeled impossible. Together, we can ensure that every child, every family, and every community have the support they deserve. Here at KOTM, our journey is far from over; we are aiming for bigger milestones and brighter futures for the families we serve, and we want you to say yes to being a part of the story.

ONE CHILD AT A TIME

*I thought the sun would never rise again. But as I look
at my boy now, I realize the sun rises with him.*

—KOTM PARENT

Raul and Laura were just like any young couple expecting their first child in 1996. Like so many young parents before them, they were equal parts eager and nervous to meet their little one. But parenthood was not the only new journey they were on. The couple had recently moved to the United States, and they were both striving to establish themselves. Working hard to make the promises of life in America a reality.

Laura's pregnancy had been typical, and everything seemed to go according to plan. However, their plan was thrown out the window when their son, Raulito, arrived prematurely. The couple did not know it at the time, but their "plan" was forever changed. In addition to the challenges that come with a preemie baby, as the days passed, it became increasingly clear that Raulito would need extensive support and care. Raulito struggled to swallow, an instinct that most babies are born with, and he continued to miss milestone after milestone.

As Raul and Laura struggled to learn a new language and attempted to navigate the labyrinth of a foreign healthcare system, they took their son to doctor after doctor, seeking answers and trying to help find the treatment he needed. As a new mom with little community support and limited access to information, Laura struggled to comprehend her son's condition fully. She admitted, "As a new mom, I had no experience with kids or babies. So for me, if he moved or didn't move, it was normal. I didn't know any different."

It wasn't until Raulito turned a year old that a doctor sat them down and finally shared with them a diagnosis: cerebral palsy. While the title offered some clarity, Laura and Raul struggled to comprehend the extent of his condition and what it would mean for Raulito's development. The hospital provided the couple with a referral for services at KOTM, but they were still unsure what "services" even meant.

When Gaby Breton, a development specialist from KOTM, knocked on the Hernandezes' door, she didn't just bring clarity and answers; she brought a lifeline. Being bilingual, Gaby bridged the language gap, connecting with the young family in their native Spanish. During that crucial first meeting, she gently guided Raul and Laura toward understanding the permanence of their son's diagnosis and disability. Until then, Raul explained, "I didn't know his condition was permanent."

Gaby understood the emotional turmoil Laura and Raul were grappling with. They were not only coming to terms with the fact their son has a disability but doing so in a strange country with very little family or friends nearby to support them. Gaby, in true KOTM fashion, stepped in to fill each of those gaps. During home visits, Gaby would often bring her own children, helping to not only foster a sense of trust between the two moms (because, let's be honest, there is a silent understanding between mothers that we just *get it*) but also allowing Laura to see first-hand how other moms parent. When their pantry seemed to be running low, Gaby would bring groceries on her next visit and restock that family's kitchen. She became a safe haven for the couple as they processed the emotional and logistical ramifications of Raulito's diagnosis.

Gaby also guided Laura and Raul through all of the programs offered at KOTM that the family could lean on, including in-person classes and therapy sessions. Laura was initially hesitant to bring Raulito to KOTM for therapy and classes, questioning why she couldn't manage his care at home.

At the time, Laura did not have a car, so making the journey across town with Raulito, who, once he was old enough, began using a wheelchair, was no small feat. She reflected, "The classes help me to get out of the house and feel that I can connect with other families, look at other resources, and start interacting with other parents." These center-based classes were so important to Laura that it was not uncommon for her to wait for the bus in the rain, snow, or sun and to then make the hour-long journey across town. Gaby nowadays often shares Laura's story with other families who struggle to make it to the center, explaining that if Laura can do it, anyone can.

Laura recounted, "It was very difficult for the first five years. Most of the time, he was in and out of the hospital with a lot of medical problems." Raulito continued to struggle with swallowing, and at one point, the doctors even recommended a feeding tube, fearing malnourishment. But Laura, bolstered by the training, support, and community of the staff and other families at KOTM, adamantly refused the feeding tube. She was unwavering in her faith that he was more than capable and that, with time, patience, and consistency, he would learn. Today, Raulito feeds himself without a hitch.

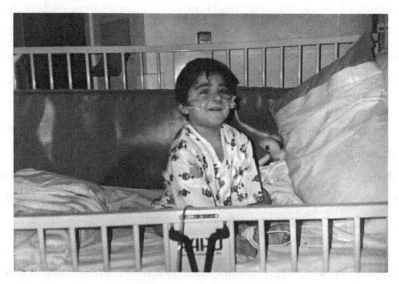

Raulito Hernandez

Laura's faith in Raulito's ability to learn and overcome the odds was more than a wish. Over the years, Raulito blossomed as the support and therapy he received had an indelible impact. The respite care program afforded the Hernandez family much-needed breaks from the round-the-clock care he required and peace of mind that Raulito was well cared for.

As Raulito's abilities grew, he continued to amaze everyone around him. Laura recalled an incident when her parents visited from Mexico. Her mother had an appointment, so before hopping into the shower, she instructed Raulito to have his shoes on and be ready by the time she returned. When she emerged from the shower, a wave of panic swept over her as nobody in the house seemed to know Raulito's whereabouts. Fearing he had wandered outside, they rushed to the front door, only to find Raulito patiently waiting by the car. Not only had he put on his shoes, but he had also maneuvered into his wheelchair, opened the garage, and even opened the car door, all to ensure they weren't late. The family was in complete shock at Raulito's newfound capabilities!

Gaby Breton explained, "Our philosophy at KOTM is to help parents, to empower parents. So when they leave us, they can know what to do with their kids." She continued, "One of my goals, since day one, is to empower families enough, and this is my good example. I empowered Laura enough that when he turned three, she knew what to do. She knew the resources that we had out in the community so that she could do it."

The Hernandez family's story is a clear illustration of the remarkable outcomes that unfold when a parent's boundless love intersects with the resources and tools needed to empower them. To this day, twenty years later, Gaby shares a close bond with the Hernandez family; Raulito and his siblings affectionately refer to her as "auntie," and she and Laura remain fast friends.

Discover the Inspiring Journey of the Hernandez Family: See How A Parent's Unyielding Support and Courage Can Empower An Entire Family Against All Odds.

chasingtheimpossiblebook.com/chapter1

It's vital to remember that Raul and Laura's story is not unique. Countless families face the unexpected challenges of raising a child with a disability. The love and support they receive make all the difference. KOTM is an organization that understands this, and its work is a beacon of hope for families like the Hernandezes, seeking much-needed information, resources, and support.

In many ways, the Hernandez family epitomizes the very reason KOTM was founded back in the 1980s. Founders Karen Hahne and Brenda Winegar, who at the time recently had become parents to children with Down syndrome, believed, despite the common assumptions at the time, that when parents are equipped with the knowledge and support, they can offer their children the brightest possible future.

FROM SMALL BEGINNINGS

"Nobody intended to start a program. That was the furthest thing from my mind," Karen Hahne recalled with a slight chuckle.

Back in 1983, Karen was a mom with a "perfect plan," just like Laura and Raul. Her own children, three of whom were adopted, were between the ages of seven and seventeen and fairly independent: everyone was potty trained and mobile. With no intentions of having any more children or adopting again, Karen was planning on returning to her career as a teacher on a part-time basis. Allowing her to work in the morning and be at home with her five children when they returned from school. It was a great plan, and everything was falling into place.

In the midst of tackling her checklist and renewing certifications, Karen received an unexpected call. It was a social worker who had the Hahnes' contact information on file from their previous adoptions. The social worker explained that a baby boy with Down syndrome was born just days before and was in need of a home. He went on to ask Karen if she would have any interest in adopting the boy. While many people in her position would politely decline or even ask for some time to consider it, Karen simply threw her plan out the window.

Before she even had time to think, Karen remembered the word "Yes" leaping out of her mouth, "In a snap moment, I just said yes. Then, the journey started. Pretty soon, I was thinking, I'm a forty-two-year-old mom; I need some help."

Just across town six years earlier, Brenda Winegar, a mom of five exceptional children, also believed she was done growing her family. Similar to Karen, her youngest son was eight, and Brenda had absolutely no plans to add another little one to the mix when she discovered that she was expecting surprise baby number six! Soon after Becca arrived, Brenda would learn that she was born with Down syndrome.

Karen Hahne and Brenda Winegar

Both Brenda and Karen, as professional teachers and experienced mothers, understood deeply the importance of education and wanted to ensure their children got the best. But, due to their child's diagnosis, they would need specialized resources if they were ever to reach their full potential. In the early 1980s, Karen and Brenda found themselves on a journey that would not only change their lives but would also light a beacon of hope for countless families. Initially seeking resources for their children with Down syndrome, they unintentionally embarked on a path that would lead them to create a place of empowerment, support, and boundless possibility for children and families facing raising a child with disabilities.

As Karen began to search for resources available for her son, Reed, she discovered PEEP (Provo Early Education Program) in Provo, Utah, which offered speech and physical therapy. But Karen quickly realized it wasn't meeting the depth of needs she envisioned for him.

When Karen first joined the program, the director pulled her aside and gently encouraged her that she needed to lower the expectations of Reed's development, cautioning her to, "Love him, but don't expect too much." She couldn't fathom accepting such limitations, especially when her heart told her there was more potential within these children than they were being credited for.

The two women's stories continued to mirror each other as Brenda was receiving similar messages. When it came to her daughter Becca's development, Brenda recalled her pediatrician cautioning her, "'Maybe Becca will be able to develop to the mental and emotional maturity of a five-year-old.' Well, I didn't like that and thought there was no way. Yes, the work would be hard, but I knew that Becca was capable of more."

But this was 1984, a time when programs for children with disabilities were few and far between. The landscape was vastly different from today without the legal protections and resources that would eventually come into play. The Americans with Disabilities Act was still six years away from being signed into law, and the journey toward equal rights was still a long and winding road.

As the two women were doing their best to take advantage of the few available programs while also looking for more options, Karen and Brenda's paths finally intersected. The two met through the Montessori school where Brenda taught. Once they connected, they quickly realized they both wanted more for their children. Would their children learn differently than typical children? Yes. But were they capable of learning? Absolutely.

Once Karen and Brenda began brainstorming how to help their kids, they knew that parent empowerment was the key. Brenda recalled, "The reason that we started our program was parent power. The parents had to have the power to be part of any kind of physical manipulation or teaching. That's what had to move. It was this parent power. We've gotta have the power if we're going to help our kids."

At Reed's next therapy appointment, Karen asked the therapist to show her how to practice the same movements so she could practice and reinforce what Reed was learning when they were at home. The therapist looked her dead in the face. "I don't work with parents," he stated bluntly.

Frustrated, Karen continued to seek out ways she could educate herself and be able to help her son. Karen learned of Pat Ollwine, a professor in Washington state who also emphasized the importance of parents as the leaders of their child's development. Karen attended a three-week-long workshop hosted by Ollwine, throughout which Ollwine continued to offer encouragement that parents know their children best and are the best ones to navigate the nuances of their care, therapy, and growth. Karen returned home emboldened, ready to dive in and take charge of Reed's education.

Upon returning from Washington at his next therapy appointment, Karen explained what she had learned and the importance of her involvement, once again asking the therapist to show her how to practice the same movements at home. This time, the therapist looked at Karen cynically and replied, "It won't work." When Karen pressed him as to why, the therapist went on, "The babies will cry, and the parents will burn out."

Undeterred, Karen insisted, "I need to know how to do this. I'm with him every day. He sees you once a week or every two weeks for 15 minutes."

Thinking back on that pivotal moment, Karen explained, "I thought, 'Babies cry anyway! And parents have a right to burn out if they're dealing with a lot of things.' It's OK to say, time out, I need some space, I need some time. So that's when Brenda and I really put our heads together and said we need to offer more, and we need to emphasize that whatever we do, the parents are there with their child."

As Reed and Becca continued to grow and enter elementary school, it was clear that expectations were going to remain low and, as a result, would potentially stunt the children's growth. How can someone learn if every teacher refuses to teach them what they are teaching the other children?

Tired of waiting on someone to help, Brenda and Karen got to work. They envisioned a place where their children could access needed therapies but also encouraged parent participation so they could replicate the techniques and exercises at home. And that is exactly what they did; they called their program Up With Downs and created a model based on what they needed.

They started slowly, and the group met wherever they could, in their homes, a local pizza parlor, borrowed office space, and even the back of an old station wagon. Despite the humble beginnings, week after week, more families joined, each seeking answers and resources. As one child developed a new skill or reached a milestone, parents would share their approach with the others so that all the children could benefit. Brenda laughed, "Once we'd started, we saw that parents appreciated coming together, talking, and sharing experiences. And if one child had developed some new skills, then another parent would say, 'What did you do? How did you get your child to do this?' There was just such strength."

Eventually, the group grew large enough to meet at the local school. And before they knew it, the need for equipment arose, which meant they would need funding. So, Karen and Brenda drove to Salt Lake City and made an appointment with the Director of Social Services. They shared with him everything they were doing with Up With Downs and petitioned him for support. They could not believe it when they walked out of his office with a check for $2,000, and with it they purchased toys, a pencil sharpener, and some chocolate!

One simple core belief continued to drive the women forward: if you empower the parents and offer support to the families, the kids will have the chance they deserve at a bright future. In a world that often fell short, they bet on hope and created the program that was clearly missing from their community. They had never run a non-profit, a community program of that size, or even parented a child with disabilities before! They did not wait until they were "qualified" or for someone's permission. They simply saw the need, said yes, rolled up their sleeves, and got to work.

Karen shared the story from those early days of a father who once felt isolated, grappling with the sudden reality of parenting a child with Down syndrome. This sense of isolation was shattered by the community they had built. Karen recounted his words, "We thought we were the only ones with Down syndrome. One day I was thinking

I was going to be playing ball in the yard with my kid, and the next day, that was gone, and I had no clue what to do or where to begin." The need for a support system was undeniable, and Up With Downs stepped in to fill that gap.

A few years later, Karen and Brenda secured their first government grant. Brenda reflected on the moment when they got the news that the grant was theirs, "Oh my gosh, we really have to do this now!" she recounted with a laugh, "There's no backing out!" She went on to share, "There was another physical therapist there that wanted to do the same thing, but we were the ones that got the grant. The therapist asked, 'You have a name?'

We replied, 'Well, no, not really.'

'I was going to use Kids on the Move.'

'That's perfect!', we practically shouted. 'Can we have it?'

He kindly replied, 'Well, I didn't get it, so yes, I'll give it to you.' And he also made space in his office. He had lots of equipment, and he offered to let us come once a week, with our group. All we could do was say thank you because we depended on prayers and the Lord. We knew we could do it if we had their help."

Since its beginnings in 1986, with seven employees serving sixty-four kids starting out, KOTM has blossomed. In 2023 alone, we served 3,110 children and employed 236 dedicated staff. The growth has been nothing short of remarkable, a testament to the unmet needs of families and the undeniable power of community. Karen and Brenda gave families more than just the words "love, but don't expect much." They bestowed upon them a sense of hope, confidence, and a path forward.

While Karen and Brenda's journey is one of triumph over adversity, it also serves as a reminder of the persistent challenges. The belief in segregating children with disabilities from society still lingers, and the struggle for recognition and investment continues. In a world that claims to have "evolved," the fight to secure resources and support for these children remains ongoing.

A KIDS ON THE MOVE MOMENT
Gaby Breton, Development Specialist

My name is Gabriela Breton, and I've been working at KOTM for over thirty-one years. It has been a great experience that has helped me grow emotionally and deeply connect with each of the families that I have known.

I remember years ago when we first moved to our building, and we only had sixty-four kids as part of our programs and seven staff. Today, we have so many staff that I don't even know how many we have, and we serve thousands of kids every month. I have had so many wonderful experiences, and it has been a joy and honor to have a front-row seat as KOTM has grown.

The beauty of my work is with the families, showing them the possibilities, helping them navigate the resources, and watching as their children grow as their family transforms. Because I have been here so long, people often ask me why I haven't explored other organizations or even different jobs. And every time, my answer is the same, I love KOTM, and my heart is here.

THE IMPACT OF PARENT POWER

Karen and Brenda were both pioneers of their time. Despite the discouragement from medical professionals and constant roadblocks, they believed that their children were capable and deserving of so much more. And they were right.

What Brenda and Karen were proposing, empowering parents and giving children with disabilities the same opportunities as their typically developing peers, was relatively new. Reed's physical therapist and his reluctance to work with Karen is evidence that even trained medical professionals were skeptical when it came to these children's potential or the parents' ability to create an impact.

While today we have studies and research that back up the effectiveness of Karen and Brenda's approach, Reed's life, in and of itself, is a testament enough. Reed was such a gifted student that while he was growing up, Karen often thought she was accidentally holding him back. Karen recounted, "Sometimes I think Reed's biggest obstacle was me because I hadn't dreamed high enough. Sometimes I bought in to what people would say about the capability of someone with Down syndrome. But as soon as I got out of his way, he proved me wrong."

When Reed was three years old, like many parents, Karen wasn't overly concerned about Reed learning to read. As a teacher she knew that would come later. "I read a lot of books to Reed." Karen recalled. "He just loved them, and we were working on learning a little baby talk sign language. But one day, one of the teachers called me into the classroom, and she said, 'You need to see this. Reed is reading!' And I replied skeptically, 'Uh, I don't think so.' And she simply replied, 'Watch.'

"As the kids came into class, the teacher had a little frame with name tags that the kids would pick up and put on as they came into the classroom. And as the kids came in, Reed would reach for each name tag and hand them to each kid. And he nailed it 100 percent!

"The whole experience just blew me away, and I kept thinking, 'OK, boy, am I behind here? He is pushing me ahead! The 'I Did It' kid has learned to read!'"

Reed Hahne

And that was simply the beginning. In 1996, Reed was nominated by his 6th grade classmates and teacher as a community hero and he was honored to carry the Olympic torch as it traveled through Utah for the Atlanta Olympics. In school, Reed was part of the National Junior's Honors Society and participated in their acapella choir and after graduating high school, he went on to attend Utah Valley University. He has served as a member of the National Youth Leadership Network, The National Down Syndrome Society where he received the Advocate of the Year Award in 2005, the Utah Developmental

Disabilities Council from 2007 to 2013, and more. He also received multiple recognitions for his service, including the Walter C. Orem award in November 2004 for his commitment to his community. As an active member of the Orem community, he has participated in over twenty-one community theater productions, including *Fiddler On The Roof* and *The King and I*. Reed has also served two missions for The Church of Jesus Christ of Latter-day Saints. Today, Reed is beginning his eleventh year as a page at the Orem Library and is a wonderful caregiver to his mom.

All of this from the young man that providers looked at and told his mother, "...don't expect too much."

Karen was dauntless in her drive to create these opportunities both for her son and every child in her community; together, they broke through the limiting expectations. And while every child and what they will one day accomplish are completely unique, Reed serves as an example that anything is possible when you believe and either find a way or are determined to make one.

Karen and Brenda did not stop at creating an organization that offers services to children with disabilities. They set a precedent early on, a precedent that has become the soul of KOTM—whenever there's a need, we step up to meet it. While KOTM's journey began with a focus on early intervention for children with disabilities and developmental delays, our vision expanded rapidly.

In the fall of 1992, to allow parents one-on-one time with their enrolled children at the center, Kids on the Move began a small Early Education Center (EEC; childcare program) for twelve children, primarily to provide care to siblings of children coming to the center for services. Several spots were also reserved for the children of staff, making it easier for them to come to work and serve the families they love. And in 2001, the EEC achieved an important milestone. They became one of the few childcare centers in the state of Utah to achieve accreditation from the National Association for the Education of Young Children.

One by one, opportunities presented themselves to serve low-income families in the community, and KOTM continued to say yes. In 1998, KOTM received a competitive grant from the federal government to provide Early Head Start services to Utah County. It is a federal requirement that 10 percent of the enrolled children in the program have a disability. We would go on to open our Autism Center, partner and soon acquire a Respite Care program, host support groups for siblings of children with disabilities, and more!

Karen explained KOTM's continued growth and expansion, "If we support the parents and we support the family, then the kids will be all right."

At no point during their tenure as CEOs of this organization did they look at a family in need and say, "That's not what we do." They chose to jump in wherever they could because they understood that when families are empowered to meet their child's needs, the kids will have their best chance at a bright future.

So, as we reflect on the journey of Karen and Brenda, let their story be a source of inspiration. Let their unwavering belief in the potential of children with disabilities and their families remind us of the transformative power of a parent's love. Their legacy calls us to challenge the status quo, to stand up for the rights and opportunities these children deserve. As a result, KOTM represents a place where empowerment, support, and boundless possibilities flourish.

A FOUNDATION FOR THE FUTURE

KOTM's dedication to meeting the needs of children never wavered as it continued to expand its programs, even when it looked impossible.

The mission remained the same—to give kids their best chance at a bright future. And after serving on the board for two years, I felt a strong pull to contribute more to ensure KOTM's long-term viability. This led me to apply for the open COO position. Drawing from my years of experience consulting with large corporations, I believed my experience could benefit KOTM. I resigned from the board and applied for the position.

My approach when consulting businesses has always been simple yet effective—identify the business value proposition, understand problems, challenges, or risks, gather data, make informed decisions, incorporate systems, build a financial plan to scale and grow, and deliver results. The challenges and complexity of operating essentially different businesses with various funding sources, each with defined, audited regulatory requirements, all within KOTM was substantial, but I knew I was the right person, with the right skills, at the right time to tackle them.

All of us, at one point or another in our lives, have a similar opportunity to use our unique skills and opportunities to create change. When that happens, it's easy to say we're too busy or that someone else can take on the challenge. However, when I looked at KOTM, I had a moment of clarity where I realized, if not me, then who? I knew, with everything inside of me, that this challenge required my experience and expertise.

So, as I took on the roles of COO and, later, CEO, my mission was clear—set up this organization for the next chapter and ensure these families have the resources they need now and in the future.

A KIDS ON THE MOVE MOMENT

Karen Hahne, Founder

Once we'd started Up With Downs, we saw how much the parents appreciated simply coming together, talking, and sharing their experiences. There was just such strength in finding a community that understands what you are walking through.

One day a woman came in and brought her baby. She shared that the baby had a brain tumor, and they knew she would not live very long. We all gathered around her to just support and love her. We told her how beautiful her baby was and what an amazing mother she was. Only one week later, the baby passed.

We received a letter from this sweet mother. In it, she shared that we were the only ones who thought her child was beautiful. At that moment, I thought to myself, "OK, this is why we're here." We have to keep going.

My first challenge as COO was to find a sustainable way to fund our Autism Center. Like most non-profits, KOTM relied solely on donations and occasional grant funding. While this had its benefits, it also had limitations. Grants often come with strict rules, and constant fundraising poses the risk of donor burnout. Government grants were not available, which had us solely relying on donations. With a significant need like that of our Autism Center, we could easily run out of necessary funding quickly.

We needed to diversify our funding sources instead of solely relying on donations. For several years, we advocated on behalf of families for insurance companies to cover autism treatment. A bill was passed in 2013, that did just that, which opened the door for us to make the game-changing decision to start billing private insurance. This decision not only made us self-sustaining but also allowed us to forecast and make decisions based on the best interests of the families we served. We weren't here to make a profit, so the additional cash flow gave us the flexibility to offer more classes and ask our families, "What do you need?" Building out programs and services based on the needs we see and not just the minimum requirements has transformed our organization. This shift allowed us to continue providing therapy and resources. We began identifying gaps in the system and actively worked toward filling them. With the Autism Center flourishing, we were better positioned to advocate for the families we served.

Today, as the CEO, the team and I are now tackling another challenge to our long-term sustainability, KOTM is in dire need of a new building and campus that provides comprehensive services for families. Keep in mind we have over 230 staff members and only sixty-four parking spaces on-site! With that in mind, it's easy to understand that when I tell you every corner of our current facility is in constant use, I am not exaggerating. This limits not only how we serve families but also how we serve our community. We've always been committed to offering our space for local events and other organizations in need, but we're currently unable to do so.

As I think about the challenge ahead, I cannot help but reflect back on KOTM's incredible journey. I am reminded that forty years ago, Karen and Brenda took a brave step to provide resources for children and their families. As we stand on the edge of monumental growth, I can say with certainty that if Karen and Brenda could step up to meet the needs of our community at their time, then we can certainly do it now.

 **YOUR MOVE**
A Rising Tide Lifts All Boats

In the United States, we are known for an approach to life commonly referred to as "rugged individualism." We value self-reliance, independence, and cheer really loudly when someone picks themselves up by their own bootstraps with no help from anyone else. While these qualities can be admirable and are worth celebrating, I can't help but wonder if we have a tendency to swing the pendulum too far in praise of rugged individualism and have forgotten the gift and blessing that is community.

Looking back on Brenda and Karen's story, I see the connecting threads between the dynamic duo and the members of the community. Almost all of them felt alone in their fight to give their child a better future. They each struggled to find needed resources and support. And when Karen and Brenda did open the "doors" to their pilot organization, Up With Downs, the families came in droves. The same families stayed when they realized they had found a place of acceptance, support, and shared learning.

For many of us, our lack of community is not all chalked up to a determination to go it alone. Towns have grown into big cities, people frequently relocate for jobs, and other factors tend to contribute to a diminishing sense of community. But with that lack of connection often comes a missing sense of responsibility and ownership in supporting and being a part of a vibrant, healthy community. I see it in my own story when I was hesitant to explore volunteering on the board of directors at KOTM. Here was an organization that was a vital part of my community, but because it didn't really align with my own needs or interests, my knee-jerk reaction was, *this doesn't have anything to do with me, so how could I be of any help?*

Yes, one independent person is capable of doing amazing things on their own. But what happens if you take ten amazing people, all highly capable, and they begin to work together? What they can create or accomplish together is going to be exponentially greater than what any of them can do on their own. We are simply stronger in numbers, and honestly, I believe we all have an innate need to be connected to one another.

In this day and age, it's easy to stay disconnected, and when the needs of the community come to our attention, we rationalize that it's not our problem. But if my time here at KOTM has taught me anything, it's that a rising tide lifts all boats. We see medical students walk through our doors as volunteers, then turn around and walk into their professions as more empathetic care providers. We see burnt-out parents get the support they need and, as a result, then thrive in their place of employment. We see children with disabilities, whom society once upon a time would have essentially thrown away, become leaders and make their communities and their world a better place.

Chances are you have directly benefited from the people who were a part of an organization like KOTM.

Whether you are hungry for connection, desiring to create a bigger impact, or potentially just curious about what it could look like to expand your world just a bit, connect with a community and find how you can serve. And if you're not sure where to start, begin with the group of people you think you have nothing in common with or are afraid of. You might just find your own version of KOTM, a place where your unique gifts are needed, and ignite the fire inside of you to be a part of something bigger than yourself.

Just as Karen and Brenda said yes forty years ago, and I said yes to joining the board, I challenge you to find your yes. So get moving because you never know who's waiting for your yes.

CHAPTER 2

FINDING HOPE

You are not alone. And even when you feel like you're alone, there's always someone who will have your back, and we'll be there for you.

—KASADI MOORE, KIDS ON THE MOVE PARENT

When Natasha Eldredge's sixth and youngest child, Grace, didn't seem to hit her milestones at the same rate as her brothers and sisters, Natasha wasn't too concerned. With five other children, Natasha was an experienced mother who knew, all too well, that each child is different. Ask any parent, and they'll confirm that every child will develop on their own time and terms.

With six children, a household to run, and a marriage on the rocks, Natasha, understandably, was a bit preoccupied and continued not to worry about her youngest, Grace. Natasha's older children kept insisting that "something is not right" and that Grace was "not able to do things like the other kids." It was this prompting that finally grabbed Natasha's attention, and she began to worry that maybe something was off with her youngest. So, she made an appointment to have Grace seen by the pediatrician.

After sharing her concerns, the doctor performed an initial screening for autism. The news was not what Natasha was hoping for: Grace was showing clear signs of ASD and would later receive an official diagnosis from a psychologist confirming the pediatrician's suspicions.

ASD is a neurological and developmental disorder that affects how people interact with others, communicate, learn, and behave. Often, kids with ASD have difficulty participating in normal, everyday activities and mastering skills that are crucial for development.

For Natasha, the news rocked her. When you realize your child can't develop independently, it can leave even the most seasoned parent feeling hopeless.

As Natasha drove home from the doctor's office, a million questions bubbled to the surface of her mind: "How can I care for her? How is she going to be independent?" She explained, "I felt responsible that she couldn't live an independent life and that somehow it was my fault. How am I going to be able to provide for her financially? Because the reality is that I'm not always going to be here. How do I keep her safe in a world that's increasingly becoming unsafe? It was very scary. It was sad. It was terrifying. It was angering."

At that point, Grace's skills and abilities were limited. She was nonverbal, which, as you can imagine, was very frustrating not only for the family but also for Grace. Taking her out in public was difficult. Natasha shared, "As a family, we couldn't go to a playground, out to eat, see a movie, anything. We could not go to a swimming pool." All the normal memories you make with your children when they are young were off the table, and Natasha didn't know if they would ever be an option. Often, the only place where Grace was content was at home, huddled in a corner with a blanket pulled over her head: a shield from the barrage of colors, lights, sounds, and other sensory stimuli that make it difficult for someone with ASD.

Natasha was referred to KOTM, where she would have access to a comprehensive array of therapies, tools, and resources Grace would need. The KOTM team at the Autism Center created a custom plan using a science-backed approach uniquely tailored to Grace's abilities and goals.

Natasha emphasized, "Remember, autism is on a spectrum, and what may be hard for one child is easy for another." Our commitment to excellent care means there is no such thing as a cookie-cutter approach to treatment. Each therapy or program is customized to work best for each child, ensuring parents, staff, and loved ones work toward the same goals. Our goal is not to check a box on a list but rather to uncover and develop what each child uniquely needs to thrive and live a full and happy life. The Eldredge family was assigned a Board Certified Behavior Analyst (BCBA) to run point on Grace's treatment, and they got to work.

The go-to treatment for those with ASD is a form of therapy called applied behavior analysis (ABA), which includes skill acquisition and behavior support. As part of her treatment plan, Grace's program included in-clinic therapy, in-home services, and parent/family training. Of course, how far or fast Grace would progress would be up to her, but Grace and her mom would have every resource they needed.

Slowly but surely, Grace began to interact with the world around her as she learned many of the skills you and I often take for granted. When she started ABA therapy, she was nonverbal, but with patience, Grace eventually found her voice. They would go to the zoo, and she would enjoy the animals. They would go to the same restaurant repeatedly, and eventually, one day, Grace ordered her own food. They went to the library, and she picked out a book she wanted. "The first time on a playground, she went over to the swings and asked another child, 'Will you play with me? Will you be my friend?' She was six.

Then, for the first time, she said, 'Thank you, mom,' and then 'I love you, Mom.' These things that we take for granted were possible because of KOTM and the caring people that you have here," Natasha shared, beaming with joy and pride.

Witness the Remarkable Journey of Grace: Experience How KOTM's Unwavering Commitment to Love and Inclusion Transformed Her Life

chasingtheimpossiblebook.com/chapter2

But Grace was not the only one learning and growing through this process. Natasha and Grace's siblings understandably had very limited exposure or understanding of ASD. That was also changing, "Throughout this process, the biggest thing that I've learned and understood is that she isn't her diagnosis. Just because there's that one area where she might have a limitation, you can find a way around it. I heard the old saying, 'If the door closes, go through a window; if the window's locked, maybe kick the door in. If there's a wall, go up, go under, go around, kick it down.' [Grace] does have this diagnosis, but it's not her, it's not her identity. She's got these limitations; there's always another area to develop strengths so that this does not have to hold her back completely." Natasha passionately explained.

Watching your child who is diagnosed with autism work diligently to learn new skills and hit those once elusive milestones is life-changing for both the parents and the child. The hope that comes with knowing that your child can, in fact, learn, grow, and thrive—not just survive—ignites a hope that was once snuffed out. Sure, they may need to "kick down a door" or learn to navigate the world a little differently, but their child CAN do it. With this understanding, a world of possibilities that parents thought were closed forever swings open again. Natasha continued, "Because of having ABA therapy, the various tools, the collaboration, and the loving and wonderful tutors that you've had here, Grace has learned not only to communicate, but the whole world has opened up. She has been able to connect."

Grace Anderson

Today, Grace is a thriving teenage girl. She can ski and paddle-board, go on rides at amusement parks, and more. Natasha then explained, "She is learning to be as independent as she possibly can, and just because she has a different wiring in her brain, let's say a different computer program running, it's not going to limit her from doing everything that she wants and living a very, very full life."

Natasha recounted a visit to a local amusement park: "Grace was nervous about going on one of the rides, asking questions about the restraints and safety. Eventually, we got on the ride, screamed the whole way, and had a blast! When we got off, she looked at me and said, 'Mom, I can do hard things.'" Natasha shared, "We call her our family's saving grace because she's just a joy to be around. She's easy to be with, full of love, very accepting, and a lot of fun!"

In addition to her contagious joy, Grace also shares her hard-earned wisdom of grit, determination, and patience with her family. Her mantra of "I can do hard things" is one she uses to inspire those around her as well. Natasha related, "A few years later, we were back at the amusement park, and this time it was my turn to be scared. Grace looked at me and said, 'Mom, you can face your fears. You can do hard things.'"[2]

UNDERSTANDING ASD AND ABA

The need for access to therapies and resources for people with ASD, or showing signs, increases every year.[3] As scientists conduct more research and we, as a society, have learned how to recognize and spot ASD, parents and communities are becoming more aware of children needing treatment. As a result, at KOTM, we have seen a rise year after year in the need for screenings and ABA therapy.

Ella Jespersen, our Autism Center Director, shares, "Some of the telltale signs of ASD are varying degrees of difficulty in social interaction, delayed verbal and nonverbal communication, and the presence of repetitive behavior and/or restricted interests. It's important to understand that no two individuals with an ASD diagnosis are the same, and therefore, how the disorder manifests and its impact on

---

2   Natasha and Grace's testimonials were solicited and their informed consent was obtained. Grace was enrolled in Kids on the Move's Autism Center from 2013 to 2018.

3   Centers For Disease Control & Prevention, "Key findings from the ADDM network | Autism | NCBDDD," CDC, March 23, 2023, accessed September 22, 2023, https://www.cdc.gov/ncbddd/autism/addm-community-report/key-findings.html.

families is incredibly unique. Because of the nature of the disorder, people with ASD often may not achieve the ability to function independently without appropriate, medically necessary treatment."

At KOTM, all therapies and interventions we use to treat ASD fall under the umbrella of ABA. ABA therapy has been used for treating autism since the 1960s. It is recognized as an effective treatment for ASD by the U.S. Surgeon General, the American Academy of Pediatrics, and the National Institute of Health. As you read in Grace's story, all ABA services at KOTM are individualized for each client and developed and supervised by a BCBA.

Because of this individually tailored approach, ABA therapy can look different depending on the learner. It often involves a lot of play and a focus on increasing language skills. It can also include working at a table, using token boards, and earning rewards. For some children, it may look like practicing daily living skills like preparing a meal, using a fork, potty training, or contributing to the home by doing chores or following a routine. Our treatments are individualized for each child based on their unique strengths and challenges.

UNVEILING ASD MYTHS

One of the most critical components to our work in the Autism Center is partnering with parents to ensure they have a scientifically based and complete picture of their child's diagnosis and treatment plan. While we have come a long way, oftentimes myths and stigmas still persist around ASD. We walk them through to a better understanding that autism is on a spectrum, and every child comes in with and without certain skills they need to work toward.

ABA therapy works to increase helpful behaviors and decrease behaviors that are harmful or affect learning. ABA therapy can increase skills across many domains, such as language, communication, attention, social skills, and daily living skills, as well as decrease problem behaviors.

We love celebrating with these families every step along the way as their kids slowly and surely, with hard work and determination, develop skills. From the first time they hear their once nonverbal child call them "mom" or "dad" or maybe, like Grace, learn to enjoy activities outside the home with their friends and family, in those moments hope is restored. While the process and timeline are different from a typically developing child, the families gain an understanding that their child *can* learn. Every milestone, no matter how big or small, is worth celebrating.

While ABA is a science, and not a "miracle," we believe it gives each child the best chance to reach their full potential, whatever that may be. By focusing on the realistic aspects of the therapy journey, we can foster a healthier understanding of the process and better support families in setting attainable goals.

Oftentimes families need to be educated on the realistic aspects of the therapy journey. ABA therapy gives each child the best chance to reach their full potential, whatever that may be, but it's not a "miracle." Unfortunately, some parents have unrealistic expectations about the outcomes, often fueled by stories of "miracles" they've encountered in books or online. Just like each treatment plan is individualized for each child, progress is very individualized as well. At KOTM we encourage each family to focus on their child's individual progress without comparing them to others. While one child may learn several new skills at once, it may take another child months of practice and hard work to learn to sign their first word of "more." We celebrate each milestone individually and honor the hard work of our clients in reaching their own individualized goals.

While we are thrilled to share Grace's story and the full life she is living now, the goal of ABA therapy is not to change an individual for the preference or convenience of a parent or anyone else. Autism isn't "bad" or something that needs to be "fixed."

ABA therapy should only be used to remediate deficits of autism that have a negative impact on an individual (for example, they engage in dangerous head-banging behavior when upset that they are told "no") and to improve the child's everyday life. It should not be used to train a child to not engage in behaviors that others may perceive as different but are otherwise not harmful. For example, we would not teach a child not to "flap their arms" because it embarrasses the parent, as the child may find a great deal of relief and coping through arm-flapping. There are characteristics of autism that make someone more unique and more wonderful than a typically developing peer, and at KOTM we celebrate each child's unique personality.

Another myth we face regularly is the belief that an ASD diagnosis will limit a child in the future. As a parent myself, I get it. Personally, there is nothing that could stop me from doing everything possible to ensure my child has the same opportunities as their peers. Parents are hardwired to fight for their children.

Also, remember that our country, the United States, does not have the greatest track record regarding ensuring equal rights for those with disabilities. It was not until 1975 when what is now known as the Individuals with Disabilities Education Act (IDEA) mandated free, appropriate public education in the least restrictive setting to children with disabilities.[4] Despite that, just over ten years later, our founder, Karen Hahne, *still* had to advocate night and day to ensure her son Reed had access to a typical classroom at school.

---

4   U.S. Office of Special Education Programs, "History of the IDEA," www.ed.gov, U.S. Office of Special Education Programs, archived, accessed September 18, 2023, https://sites.ed.gov/idea/files/idea-history.pdf.

Between historical precedence, inherited misinformation, and a sea of "advice" on the internet, parents are often facing a barrage of myths. So it's no wonder many parents are worried that a diagnosis like ASD, ADHD, or others will prevent their child from accessing a typical education and limit their options in the future for careers. By gently educating not only every child but every family, we can bust these myths, empower their kids, and learn to celebrate the seemingly small successes for the mountain-top achievements they really are. Empowering children with ASD with the skills needed to navigate the world requires endless hard work and dedication, but we know that they can do it.

A KIDS ON THE MOVE MOMENT
Kellie Hunsaker, Clinical Director and BCBA

When I began my career, I wanted to help kids communicate. I feel like there's a huge lack of emphasis on communication for children. I was going to be a Speech Language Pathologist when I realized I wanted to help kids' lives improve on a higher level and that the work of a BCBA was a better fit. I want to help in every way: communication, daily living skills, and more.

My passion comes from seeing the little small improvements that kids make. The very first child I worked with at KOTM was a little girl who couldn't talk or walk or use her hands or anything. It was really amazing to be able to give her an opportunity to connect with the help of a communication device. Even though that improvement was so small and minimal, she could finally address her mom. And for the first time, her mom could see, "Oh, she knows who I am." We can

CHAPTER 2: FINDING HOPE

make these little teeny improvements in kids' lives that have bigger outcomes than parents thought their child would ever have.

Progress with children with autism is very slow. Often, people get impatient and frustrated that the improvements aren't happening fast enough. It's a huge barrier that we overcome all the time, and we have to offer lots of encouragement, for example, "I know your kiddo is not talking yet, but he pointed. That's pretty cool."

We have to work with parents and set the expectation that this progress is slow and it will take time to see the change they are hoping for. Just because a kiddo's behavior isn't fixed overnight or even in a year doesn't mean everyone wasn't really, really working very hard on trying to change it. There are kids in our Autism Center who have been here for eight years, and they're still working on skills. And that is OK! These things take time.

To the parents out there who are facing an autism diagnosis, I want you to know that there are lots of people who are going to help you. Once you find those people, they're going to help steer your ship, and once we get things figured out, your ship's gonna sail smoothly from there.

EARLY INTERVENTION MATTERS

In the first seven years of life, a child's mind is a massive sponge and they are essentially building skills one on top of the other. For example, skills that a baby masters when it learns to crawl are used when they learn to play t-ball. When a child has ASD, it usually means they have skipped a skill, and through ABA therapy they need to backtrack and develop that skill. The younger a child is when they go back and learn these skills, the easier it is for them and the more permanent the skill becomes. This is why it's so important for a child to have access to early intervention and therapy in the first three years of life. Unfortunately, there are several barriers that often prevent many families from enrolling in an early intervention program.

Children with ASD usually begin exhibiting signs between the ages of eighteen months and two years. Sometimes, a skill regression is a signal; for example, they were talking, and now they are not. Other times, it's a social behavior, such as not looking someone in the eye. Most of the time, these signs can be very subtle. So, when you're part of a busy family like Grace is, and given that every child develops differently, it's easy for a caregiver to delay having their child evaluated. One child previously in our program, Varrick Moore, would refuse to look his father in the eye, starting when he was little. His father assumed it was simply because he was a baby, and like many children when they are small, was more attached to his mother.[5]

Explore the Moore Family's Journey: Discover How Community Support and Unwavering Hope Help Them Embrace Life with Autism.

chasingtheimpossiblebook.com/chapter2

Another delay to early intervention is an official diagnosis, which can only be given by medical doctors trained to treat ASD; including child psychiatrists, pediatric neurologists, or developmental pediatricians as well as trained specialists who are not medical doctors such as child psychologists. Without this diagnosis, services are typically not covered by private insurance. The waitlist to see a psychologist in the state of Utah is usually between nine and twelve months. This means that even if a child does begin exhibiting signs right at eighteen months old and it's immediately caught by caregivers, that child can still miss out on that critical early intervention window because they are waiting on an official diagnosis.

But the wait does not end there. Once a child has been identified as having ASD and officially diagnosed, there is often another waitlist for a BCBA. These highly trained and credentialed professionals are key to effective ABA therapy. They can effectively complete an assessment with a recommended treatment plan to determine how many skills a child should have and then work toward building the missing skills. Also, you must work with a BCBA if you want insurance to cover the cost of treatment. A BCBA can only reasonably carry a caseload of about twelve to fourteen clients, and there are less than six hundred of these professionals in the entire state of Utah and less than fifty-two thousand in the United States.[5]

To give you a sense of the large need for these services, currently, our Autism Center serves about 165 children annually, which is our current capacity. But if we were to serve *everyone* who calls or reaches out to us needing therapy for their child with ASD, it would amount to over 400 children every year! In just the state of Utah, 1 in 27 eight-year-old boys and 1 in 85 eight-year-old girls have autism.[6] Additionally, the need here in Utah is greater as Utah also has one of the highest birth rates in the United States. As of 2021, the birth rate

---

5   Kasadi and Varrick's testimonials were solicited and their informed consent was obtained. Varrick was enrolled in Kids on the Move's Autism Center from 2017 to 2021. Behavior Analyst Certification Board, "Region-specific certificant data," BACB, accessed September 21, 2023, https://www.bacb.com/services/o.php?page=101134.

6   Matthew J. Maenner, "Prevalence and characteristics of autism spectrum disorder among children aged 8 years—autism and developmental disabilities monitoring network, 11 sites, United States, 2020 | MMWR," CDC, March 24, 2023, accessed September 21, 2023, https://www.cdc.gov/mmwr/volumes/72/ss/ss7202a1.htm?s_cid=ss7202a1_w.

in Utah was 14.0 per 1,000 residents; this is higher than any other state as well as the nation's average of 11.0 births per 1,000 people.[7]

Given each of these obstacles, many families can easily miss out on a year, or possibly even two, of early intervention services due to no fault of their own. At KOTM, we know that taking advantage of these sponge years is critical to building those initial skills. We're now in the beginning stages of exploring ways we can eliminate these wait times and expand our capacity to serve more families. From working to have a psychologist on site who can provide a needed diagnosis to offering mentoring and developing master's students who are pursuing their BCBA certification, we are examining all the possibilities with the knowledge that these kids can't wait.

THE HIGH COST OF HOPE

In 1998, Cheryl was a busy mom of three happy and healthy children. Like most mothers in the 1990s, ASD was nowhere on her radar. But then she noticed something different about her youngest son, David. Cheryl explained, "He had a few speech words, and he dropped them. And I thought that was kind of weird. And then he started doing some weird behaviors at about eighteen months old, running down the hall with his eyes sideways, then hitting the wall repetitively." Cheryl connected with their family doctor and David was eventually referred to a speech therapist. Everyone believed he would eventually catch up and the case would be closed.

When David was three, the family relocated to a neighboring town, and with that move, they began working with a new speech

---

7   Maja Josifovska, "What is the average size of an American family: statistics & facts," TestHut.com, May 16, 2023, accessed February 22, 2024, https://www.testhut.com/average-size-of-an-american-family-statistics/.

therapist. After their first session together, the speech therapist asked Cheryl to fill out a questionnaire. Both mother and therapist were able to identify the true source of David's speech difficulties, and he was soon after diagnosed with ASD.

At that time, there was so little understood about autism. In the year 2000, only 51 percent of the population owned a home computer, and we were still a few years away from the dawn of smartphones.[8] So, opening up a search browser and typing in your child's symptoms was not the common practice as it is today. Like many people at the time, Cheryl's only reference for ASD was Dustin Hoffman's character in the movie *Rain Man*. I cannot imagine how isolated and lost she felt.

David's doctor was incredibly helpful in helping Cheryl find resources and books to read, but support was limited. David continued speech therapy and was also enrolled in occupational therapy. Still, it would be another full year before they could get off the waitlist and start ABA therapy at a local program. Yet when David was in elementary school, the special ed class did not have the focus on ASD that David required. So Cheryl decided to send him to school the first half of the day, and the second half of the day a private therapist would come to their home and do ABA therapy with David.

Every therapist, every program, and every session was one hundred percent Cheryl and her husband's responsibility to pay for. Cheryl shared, "It was all out of pocket. Probably ended up costing us $40,000 for just, I don't know, a couple of years. It just tapped us out." Eventually, Cheryl and her husband would drain their savings and all retirement funds to cover the high cost of David's treatment.

---

8   *New York Times*, "Report counts computers in majority of U.S. homes," (*New York Times*, September 7, 2001, accessed September 22, 2023, https://www.nytimes.com/2001/09/07/us/report-counts-computers-in-majority-of-us-homes.html.

While the year 2000 may not feel like that long ago for some of us, it was a time when private insurance covered less for ASD treatment than they do now. Billing insurance simply was not an option. A few years ago, we piloted a Medicaid Autism Waiver Program in an attempt to work with the legislature to get private insurance to start covering treatment. Our local legislature had been listening to our community, including the team at KOTM, parents, and other organizations, as we advocated that the cost of this treatment should be covered. If private insurance was not going to do it voluntarily, we needed our representatives to step in.

In response, the government offered a Medicaid waiver as a pilot program. Our goal was to work with legislatures to gather the necessary data and information needed for Medicaid to cover treatment so that they could then turn it into a format that could be used for private insurance. Essentially doing the footwork of providing the framework for billing to private insurance, private insurers could not use the lack of framework as an excuse not to cover treatment. This, in turn, would prevent private insurers from denying expensive treatments and filing them as unnecessary.

The government allocated about half a million dollars for the pilot. They outlined certain requirements for tracking a child's progress, such as the work done in a session and the benefits they were experiencing. The program was immensely successful. Thanks to KOTM and the other programs that participated in the waiver pilot, the legislature was able to use the data compiled from that program to make sound decisions and really advocate for private insurance to cover the costs.

Today, billing private insurance will typically cover a portion of a child's needed therapy. Still, for many parents the costs, in the price of therapy, lost wages due to time away from work, and high insurance deductibles, are a barrier to getting their child the therapy they need.

Here at KOTM, we offer donor assistance, payment plans, and bill insurance to help keep out-of-pocket costs down for families, but we are not stopping there. We continue to be an advocate in reducing costs wherever possible.

A KIDS ON THE MOVE MOMENT

Courtney Mitchell, Assistant Clinical Director and BCBA

I didn't go into my first job with kids with autism knowing that I'd become so passionate about it. I was in my undergrad, and to be honest, my major was psychology, and I just wanted to do something in the mental health field. But working with these kids and seeing the progress they could make and the hope and joy it brings to families when there is progress really makes me feel like I'm making a difference. It brings me just as much joy as it does the children when they make progress.

First and foremost, I always want to ensure that kiddos feel safe and respected. With ABA, yes, we do focus on behavior change, but I only want to change something that is socially significant and not just change someone to fit in with what society says. I want to help kids be the best version of themselves that they can be. So I make sure that their individual personality and what's important to them stays with them and stays true to them.

It's important that we're listening to the child's consent. So if they're not OK with something we're doing, we stop and we reassess. We make sure that we're helping the children progress in a way that they want to progress, rather than how only a parent or a clinician or society says they should be progressing.

I am incredibly proud to be able to work with so many different kids who no longer need services and are able to be independent. Our goal is always to help kids so they don't need our services anymore. So when a child is able to graduate or be successful without our help anymore, that's the end goal.

FINDING HOPE IN SMALL VICTORIES

Obtaining an ASD diagnosis for a child can provide parents with a road map to help their child, but it often does not alleviate the shock and guilt they all too often navigate. Parents often wonder if their child's diagnosis resulted from something they did or if it's somehow their fault. Daily, we see parents who beat themselves up for not noticing the signs sooner and getting their child help faster. And all of this guilt is compiled by the grief that comes when the future you once imagined for your family and your child is forever altered.

But something truly magical happens when a family starts to see their child achieve a milestone. Maybe it's the first time a mother hears her child's voice call out "mom" or say "I love you." Or it could be the moment they easily eat a food with a texture they normally don't like. At that moment the miracle is not necessarily the reaching of the milestone, but rather it's the moment hope comes back into the picture. That sense of peace that is born from knowing your child will be OK begins to grow inside of a parent once again.

They are finally able to see a light at the end of the tunnel, because, while it may be slow, growth is possible, and learning is possible. A world of possibilities is restored because they know their child is going to find their own unique way to navigate the world with courage and curiosity. Every family navigating ASD deserves this life-giving hope.

YOUR MOVE
The Underestimated Power of Kindness

There is a huge demand in our community for more services. From getting a diagnosis to finding a certified BCBA with an opening in their caseload, assistance with covering the high cost of treatment, and more, the need is bigger than ever, but we refuse to believe meeting these needs is impossible. Here at KOTM, part of the plan for our building's expansion is a state-of-the-art facility and center of excellence which can meet these needs and do so under one roof, which I will share more about in a later chapter. If you're able, we will, of course, welcome any amount of financial support that will allow us to extend hope to more families.

But there is also a larger need that every single one of us can work to meet, and that is the need for more grace, more understanding, more kindness, and more patience for families and children with ASD. Children with ASD process the world differently than a typical person. So, a loud noise that may be a small annoyance to you or me could be completely overwhelming for a person with ASD. A joyful social gathering, like a family cookout, might be fun for everyone else, but it can mean several hours of crushing anxiety that a child with ASD has to find a way to navigate.

Grace's mother, Natasha, said it so well, "Don't be so quick to judge. If you see my child with a blanket over her head or she's down on the floor and she's screaming, don't automatically say, 'Oh, your child's a brat, or you're a bad parent.' Understand that this child may be having a lot of these sensory overload issues, and that parent is doing the best that they can." If you see a child having a meltdown, being combative with a parent, or refusing to participate, choose kindness before you jump to a conclusion. Have patience for these children and their caregivers, who are doing their best to guide them through a world that, at that moment, makes no sense.

Kindness is a move we can all make.

CHAPTER 3

CARE

Honestly, seeing these kids all interact with people different from them and being unfazed is worth it. I think my kids see the world differently because of their Kids on the Move experience. If they just lived in our neighborhood and our specific area, they probably wouldn't have that same exposure. I honestly think they will face the world in a different, more beautiful way because they see and appreciate differences. And I don't know, it's not like the one solution to all of our communities' problems, but I think it's a solution.

—DEVIN PATTEN, PRESCHOOL AND CHILDCARE PARENT

On a snowy December morning in 2018, a miracle came into the world. After a grueling thirty-six-hour labor and delivery aided by forceps, Kohen Killen made his appearance. He was only thirty-six weeks old, but at 6 lbs and 21 inches, they could already tell he was a fighter. His parents, Emilie and Johnny, were thrilled, and in those first few moments as a family of three, all seemed right with the world. Unfortunately, this moment of perfection would not last.

As they were snuggled together while doctors and nurses performed their routine checks, it soon became clear something was wrong with little Kohen. The doctors quickly whisked Kohen away for observation. Just a few days later, as Emilie was discharged from the hospital, Kohen was admitted to the NICU. From episodes where he would suddenly stop breathing to eventually uncovering a brain bleed, Kohen remained in the NICU for twenty-one days while doctors supported his little body. Thinking back on those twenty-one days of waiting, hoping, and watching, Emilie shared, "Every day is torment; you go one step forward one day, and the next day it feels like ten steps back."

During Kohen's stay in the NICU, Emilie and Johnny had to transform from being new parents to overnight experts in neurosurgery, hematology, and more as they attempted to keep up with one specialist after another who tried to identify the source of Kohen's condition. Emilie explained, "We had to consider, is this a viral thing? Was this seizure-induced? He would have a seizure every two or three days, which then they call on a whole fleet of doctors, and you get reeducated on everything."

When Emilie and Johnny finally did get the chance to bring Kohen home, it was without a clear diagnosis or clear path forward. But they were discharged with a whole list of referrals, including one for KOTM. A few days later, a KOTM team member reached out with information on their early intervention services, but at that point, the overwhelmed couple wasn't sure what they needed or if Kohen even fit into any of the programs.

Eventually, the Killen family did receive a diagnosis for Kohen, congenital hydrocephalus. Extra fluid on his brain was not draining properly, causing the ventricles to grow larger and create immense pressure. Doctors moved quickly to place a shunt in three-month-old Kohen's small body.

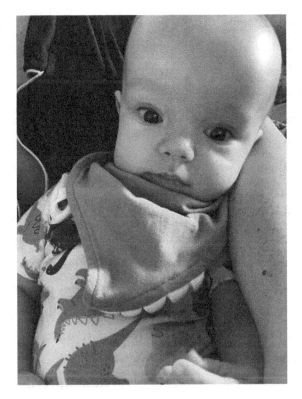

Kohen Killen

After surgery, Emilie and Johnny saw a night-and-day difference in their little miracle. He was suddenly an incredibly content and happy baby who no longer needed pain medication. The ease in his demeanor and the relief that he was stable allowed the Killen family to settle into their own sweet version of normal. It also allowed them to see that Kohen was, understandably, behind in his milestones. It was then that they knew they could reach out to KOTM for support to get Kohen where he needed to be developmentally.

Almost immediately, the new parents could tell a big difference between the providers they had been working with versus the team at KOTM. The care teams at hospitals and doctor's offices would often talk *at* the couple, Emilie explained, "You kind of hear the buzzwords like, 'physical therapy,' 'O.T.,' 'possible autism.' But you don't really know what they mean." In the light of tackling one emergency after another, these words didn't carry as much weight in those first few months before Kohen received his shunt.

But working with the KOTM staff was a collaborative discussion, and the couple felt for the first time that someone was taking the time to educate them on what was happening with their son and empower them to make an informed decision. The couple was able to understand the purpose of early intervention and the possible outcomes. Emilie continued, "Some kids do early intervention and go on and are totally fine. Some kids do early intervention, and it's exactly the thing they need. Some kids do early intervention, and then we can target specifically what they need to help them develop the proper way."

The Killens also saw that the KOTM team was willing to take Emilie and Johnny's expertise as Kohen's parents and blend it with their expertise as medical professionals to create a plan that was exactly what Kohen needed. This approach immediately broke down their barriers. While they initially had felt like early intervention was a box their child was being placed in or as punishment for them as parents not doing enough, they came to see that no one was pointing fingers at them and that they, instead, had a partner in KOTM.

As a new parent, you're never entirely sure when your child is supposed to hit milestones, but the Killens were also trying to factor in Kohen's experiences: extended NICU stay, seizures, and surgery. But with the support of the KOTM team, they could rest assured that Kohen would eventually get where he needed to be in his own time. Yes, Kohen was slow to make all of his milestones—he was late to crawl, didn't walk until after he turned two, and had trouble swallowing his food, but having the backup of his early intervention team to encourage and guide Emilie and Johnny was huge. Kohen joined the Early Intervention program when he was four months and remained a part of the program until he was three and transferred to the school district for his care.

Not long after his transfer, changes in their family dynamic would require Emilie to return to work. She had been providing full-time care for Kohen since birth, with only the occasional help from family members. Finding a daycare is an emotional process for any parent, especially when you are their only caregiver, but it can be terrifying when you layer in your child's special needs. The Killens' search criteria for a daycare consisted of what every parent looks for—a happy, bright, cheerful place with engaging staff and a small child-to-adult ratio. Unfortunately, as many parents discover, those places are hard to find and even harder to get into.

Faced with a scary situation, they didn't know what to do; they couldn't just put Kohen into a regular daycare. Sure, Kohen was growing more and more capable each day, but with speech delays, a shunt, and other factors, he still had special needs. Johnny outlined, "Here are two parents who have to go back to work and leave their child that still can't really talk, can't really walk, and needs help still eating."

Emilie added, "We have to trust somebody with our unique child and his unique situation, and who could do that?"

The stakes were simply too high to place him in childcare and hope for the best.

After driving around all day, looking at over twenty daycare facilities, the couple realized they happened to be close to the KOTM campus. They had received all their therapy services from KOTM in their home, so they had never seen the facility before. At that moment, Johnny remembered KOTM had a childcare program and suggested they stop by and check it out.

Emilie pushed back; she was exhausted from a long, emotionally draining day, and the last thing she wanted to see was another childcare facility that would disappoint her. Johnny insisted they check it out and pulled into the parking lot. Emilie shared, "We walked into KOTM, and I hadn't talked to anybody, but all of a sudden, I felt at home." They decided on the spot to sign Kohen up for childcare. The application and enrollment process was smooth, and the next day, they got a call that Kohen had been accepted.

The new schedule and routine were an adjustment for the whole family. At first, as many toddlers do, Kohen was upset when Emilie would drop him off on her way to work. The teachers continued to reassure Emilie and Johnny that they were taking great care of Kohen and that everything would be OK. Emilie beamed, "They just gave us the confidence to keep bringing him back and trust that it's going to work out. It's always gut-wrenching to leave your child, but there is peace when it's simply because you're going to miss your child, and you're not scared that their needs are not being met." Within a few days, Kohen was feeling right at home and was spending his time at the KOTM childcare center laughing, playing, and learning alongside his new friends.

Kohen was enrolled in KOTM childcare from April until December of that year. Unfortunately, once again, one December morning, things took a turn for the worse, and Johnny and Emilie were at the mercy of doctors once again to save their son. Diagnosed with pneumonia, sweet Kohen was incredibly ill, and doctors admitted him to the hospital. While he was fighting for his life, his KOTM family did not forget about Kohen. The teachers and his friends in daycare would constantly send messages, songs, and crafts to let Kohen know they were cheering for him. Soon, his hospital room was filled with paper flowers and sweet crayon drawings, signs of just how much he was loved and missed. Emilie remembered, "It felt like all of them were on the journey with us."

For a month and a half, Kohen fought bravely. Between antibiotics, intubation, and eventually being placed on an ECMO machine, his health continued to pendulum swing; just as he would start to get better, he would then get worse. Eventually, his body was weakened and damaged from pneumonia, a stroke, and the different treatments. Kohen was just too weak to keep fighting and, this time, did not come home.

The love that Kohen's parents and the entire team at KOTM had for him continues to endure. After his passing, KOTM arranged a special celebration of little Kohen's life. Marj Crowther, our Director of Preschool and Childcare, knew just how much Kohen loved being outside and suggested planting a tree in his honor. Emilie shared, "That offering meant so much to us because it showed us how much KOTM really cared for our son. Not just while he was here, but after, and will still care about him going forward."

Step Into the World of the Killen Family: Witness Their Journey of Love, Loss, and Resilience, and See How KOTM Played an Essential Role in Their Lives.

chasingtheimpossiblebook.com/chapter3

We are so incredibly honored and grateful that we had the opportunity to love on and be a part of Kohen's life. That while he was part of our childcare program, we could support his parents and create a safe, happy, wonderful place for Kohen to learn and grow each day. At KOTM, we believe that every parent and every child deserves access to this holistic approach to childcare. As Emilie described childcare at KOTM, "We can drop our kid off at daycare and know 100% that he's going to be cared for, looked after, loved, and protected. And that's going to make me a better person because I can then go into the world and do my job more effectively and efficiently, knowing that I have the best people looking after our kid."

A KIDS ON THE MOVE MOMENT
Lacey Wilson, Preschool and Childcare Assistant Director

After being a part of KOTM for twenty-two years, I think one of the things that makes our childcare facility so special is its uniqueness. I've had the opportunity to tour a lot of other facilities for training but also in looking for ideas on how we can raise the quality of care. A lot of childcare facilities do not have an inclusive program.

I love how inclusive our childcare is, and how special it is to know the children here are treated as equals. Our kids learn how to treat those who are different, whether it's due to disabilities or something else like a language barrier. We have kids who don't speak English: Russian, Chinese, Japanese, Spanish, and others. We take the time to help them grow, and our children learn that everybody's different and to love them for their uniqueness.

Knowing that I've made a positive impact on the children that have come to the center has meant the world to me. For some it's an impact that has lasted for years—I'm still in contact with some of my students from when I first started. They're serving [church] missions, or they're getting married—and still talk about the positive impact and influence that me and the other staff members have had on them.

In my time here, I am amazed at how much we have grown and that the need for our services is so prevalent. And it's nice to know that, as a whole, KOTM has an impact on our culture, on our community. When people talk about KOTM, it's usually a very positive experience, whether they themselves or someone they know used our services.

I am absolutely amazed that we went from serving just a couple hundred kids at the beginning, to now, in the thousands, and it's only going to grow. We have so much dedication within our staff that it keeps growing and we're able to serve our community more, not just here in the center, but all over the place.

MORE THAN CHILDCARE

At KOTM, we believe childcare can and should be more than a place you have to stick your child and pray they are OK while you go to work. Every child deserves a place where they are seen, and known, not simply watched while their parents work. Every parent deserves the peace of mind of knowing their child is truly loved and cared for, not just another head that needs to be counted.

Our Preschool and Childcare program takes both children with disabilities and typically developing children. At most childcare facilities, if a child is not potty trained or is nonverbal, or like Kohen, has a shunt and speech delays, they are often turned away. We never turn away a child because of a special need. Can you imagine a parent's frustration, anger, and despair when they MUST work to put food on the table, but no childcare facility will enroll their child? It's the reality for thousands of families across the United States every single day.

Like many of our programs at KOTM, our childcare center opened because we saw a need and made moves to meet it. Our founders, Karen and Brenda, realized that many of the teachers and therapists which were employees at KOTM had limited availability for sessions because they were also full-time mothers, and could only work when their partner was home. Karen and Brenda realized that if onsite childcare were an option, they would have more ability to teach and offer sessions.

Also, onsite childcare would provide a place for siblings to hang out while a parent attended classes or therapies with their disabled brother or sister. A preschool and childcare facility meant that anyone, whether client or therapist, could keep their kids safe and close while knowing they were well cared for. It just made sense, and the childcare program launched in the fall of 1992 as the Early Education Center (EEC).

A PLACE THAT FEELS LIKE HOME

When you walk into our childcare building, it feels nothing like the well-worn daycare down the street. No, we wanted the place to feel like home. You enter into a beautiful reception and are greeted by two sweet parakeets—all the children love saying hello to the birds, Sunshine and River, when they arrive. To the right is our expansive library of beautifully illustrated and fun books for the little ones, and shelf upon shelf of resources for parents. A convenient key card security system gives direct access to the childcare wing of the building and ensures every child's safety. The classrooms are decorated with warm, neutral colors that give a calming feeling, and there are plenty of toys for every child to enjoy. Large windows bring the outdoors in, and beautiful treatments make the rooms serene, cool, and dim for nap times. Two-way mirrors can offer peace of mind to parents who are nervous about leaving their little ones and want to stay behind for a few moments to watch. Each room has easy access to the playground for lots of sunshine and exploring. And our program director is actively involved in each classroom, offering nurturing and loving support.

Marj Crowther, our Director of Preschool and Childcare, shared, "We are unique in the sense that we work hard to ensure the social and emotional well-being of a child. It's proven that if a child is well-adjusted socially and emotionally, they'll do better academically. But if they don't have that foundation of social and emotional well-being, everything is hard. It's a vantage point from which our teachers guide the children. We honor the children; we know that they have ideas and feelings. Those feelings are often big, and we value those feelings.

"Children's feelings get overlooked in a typical childcare, but we see them, and we know that just because they're little doesn't mean they don't have big feelings. We honor that, and then it creates a domino effect, like a good thing that just spreads throughout the whole classroom. It's one of those unspoken, unseen things that take place as a byproduct of just modeling behavior."

EVERYONE WINS

Our Preschool and Childcare is one of six programs we offer at KOTM at the same location. While our EEC was originally created for the KOTM staff and parents of enrolled children, we have expanded, providing services for all families who are in need of childcare in the community, including typical children. Naturally, due to our expertise, we receive a higher than usual percentage of children with disabilities in our childcare.

One of the unique offerings that we are focused on is comprehensive care. For example, if a child had an autism diagnosis, a parent can drop their child off in the morning and in the afternoon we will walk the child over to our Autism Center for three hours of ABA therapy three days a week, and the other two days a week we take them to our Family Support Services to receive one hour of speech therapy, then bring them back to the childcare center. Instead of the parent making multiple appointments driving around the valley, missing work and coordinating appointments, they can have all the services needed to support their child during the day at KOTM while they are at work. We are extremely unique and revolutionary in the way we support families.

In addition to the benefits the kids receive from being in a nurturing and inclusive environment, it's a huge benefit to our staff and community. About 85 percent of the KOTM employees are female; this is in part due to their ability to have onsite childcare. Between scarcity of options, absorbent costs, the wage gap, and rising inflation, many women simply cannot afford childcare—which makes it all the more important that we provide it for our employees at a reduced cost.

And because all the services we offer at KOTM are under the same organization, we can continue to support the needs of the family outside of childcare. For example, if there is a child enrolled who is beginning to exhibit early signs of autism or behavioral problems, we can have one of our onsite BCBAs observe and, if needed, make a recommendation to the parents on the next steps. Early intervention then becomes all that much more of a possibility.

We know turnover can be traumatic for children, so we do everything possible to retain our amazing staff. This means giving consistent raises and bringing more qualified hands into the classroom for support. We often partner with nursing students needing to log volunteer hours, and they serve as a teacher's aide in the classroom.

Our financial goal is not to make money; we're thrilled if we can break even. Our purpose is solely to serve our staff, families, and communities with desperately needed high-quality childcare.

About 30 percent of the children in our childcare program have disabilities and developmental delays. But they are never sidelined or kept apart from the typical children. Everyone learns, plays, and grows together. As they learn side by side, these children build acceptance of others who are different from them, facilitating a much greater understanding of what they have in common rather than differences. There is a higher level of compassion with the kids as every day these children learn to treat one another with respect and kindness.

Marj shared an example of this in action:

"Tommy has Down syndrome, and so he does look different than the other children. And I don't believe Bobby had ever been around any children with Down syndrome.

They were all out on the playground, playing and hiding in a tunnel together. Bobby said to the other children, 'Come on guys, he's weird.' pointing at Tommy. 'Let's not play with him. Let's go over here and play.'

Their teacher heard the conversation, walked over, and said gently, 'Bobby, yes, Tommy looks different, and he can't help the way he looks. We respect him just like we respect you. So because of that, we're all a family, and we want to all play together.'

Just then, Johnny chimed in, 'Come on, Bobby, we're all friends. We're all learning how to be good friends!' And from there, all the children went off and played together, Tommy included."

The compassion these kids learn is truly remarkable.

When sweet Kohen was in the hospital, one of his playmates approached the teacher and said, "We need to pray for Kohen's parents." To have such emotional intelligence and compassion at a young age is a gift. Imagine where we could be as a community and a culture if everyone had learned this level of compassion and kindness when they were in preschool.

Marj went on to share, "While our services in and of themselves are vital and important, we're not just providing childcare, we are hopefully creating, modeling, and teaching a more inclusive community."

A KIDS ON THE MOVE MOMENT
Carley Scalora, Preschool and Childcare Parent

My son Calvin, who's six, and I spent pretty much all of our time together when he was younger due to his medical complexities. And, of course, COVID-19 contributed quite a bit to how much we stayed home. So, I was really nervous about letting him go to daycare.

We have been with KOTM since he was three months old. He did the early intervention program where they came to our house—he did occupational therapy, physical therapy, speech, all of his therapies. When he was almost three, we did motor class, the learning box and all your preschool prep. We were sad thinking we were done.

I looked for a long, long time for childcare, trying to find a place that I could trust and that Calvin would enjoy. Also, it needed to be someone who would work with our unique medical situation. I kind of felt like we were at the end of our rope until I remembered KOTM. I found the childcare program and we were so happy to come back. Everybody here loves Calvin, appreciates us, and was willing to work with us. Since we already knew it was a place that was safe, and he liked it, it made it very easy to send him.

The fact that the childcare program takes all kids, and that they're willing to make accommodations, made it easy to trust the program.

Calvin has grown exponentially from simply being around other kids that understand him. I think it's important for children to be exposed to different abilities so when they're out in the real world they have these experiences to draw on. It's something they have seen before, and suddenly that child with a different ability from theirs is just another kid who wants to play.

Carley and Calvin Scalora

Calvin also benefits from time to himself when mom's not there—he can kind of figure out who he is outside of home. He's gotten a lot braver and is learning how to socialize more.

The staff are continuously learning about different kinds of behaviors and disabilities in order to meet each kid's needs. Many places are very cookie cutter: "This is what we do for each kid." But Calvin doesn't always fit those molds, so I love that KOTM works with typical kids and neurodiverse kids, and brings them all together. They're always learning and growing, and it's just a magical place. We love it here.

Join Carley's Journey of Hope and Resilience: See How Inclusive Education Empowered Calvin and Provided a Pathway to Overcoming Fear.

chasingtheimpossiblebook.com/chapter3

YOUR MOVE
Excellent Childcare for All

When I was a young mom, I had no idea how critical the first seven years of a child's life are for their development. The way we speak to children and teach them how to express their feelings and emotions creates an impact for the rest of their lives. This is why it matters what kinds of experiences they have in childcare. As a mother myself, I recognized early on what a profound impact caregivers and teachers had on my children. My children loved and adored them.

One of the biggest needs we have right now is funding that will allow us to hire more support in each classroom. Marj explained,

> "One of the problems is the teachers get burned out very quickly. Due to the needs of their children, they have to be hyper attentive all the time, and there is no downtime. You can't avoid burnout under these types of circumstances, but if we had enough teachers that we could pull from their strengths for a particular situation, be fluid and move them back and forth in order to be supportive of everything that goes on in the classroom.... Oh my goodness! The children would get the best of the best!"

At KOTM it's our honor and privilege to provide a safe, warm, inclusive, and caring environment where every child feels known and seen. Whether they are with us for a few years, or, like Kohen, only a few months, every parent deserves the peace that comes with knowing their child is loved while at childcare.

And while we can't fix how every daycare is run, at KOTM we can expand our capacity to serve children with excellence. We need subsidized funding or donations so we can continue to lower the teacher-to-student ratios without financially burdening their parents. We want to support staff in all capacities and continue outfitting each classroom with the staff and resources needed for those specific children, making each room even more inclusive.

I suspect that many of the people reading this book are business owners, C-suite executives, and influential leaders within your companies. If that's so, chances are high that a large percentage of your work force are parents and even higher that you do not provide onsite childcare for your employees. If that is the case, I'd like to challenge you to consider offering high-quality, inclusive, onsite childcare for your employees or at least some sort of childcare benefit.

While many companies assume that the cost is too high, the data proves that it's just good business. Companies that offer childcare benefits see a reduction in absenteeism, have higher retention rates and see an increase in productivity, and attract top tier talent.[9]

If you're a parent with a child in a daycare program or private school, another move you can make is to advocate for the program to become more inclusive for children with disabilities. While it is illegal to turn away a child with a disability, many centers or schools will put arbitrary rules or restrictions in place that automatically disqualify

---

9   Shilpa Gaidhani, "Employer Sponsored Child Care Program," *International Journal of Advance Research and Development* 3, no. 3 (2010): 78–85.

children with disabilities. For example, many preschool programs will outline that a child must be completely potty trained by the age of three in order to be enrolled, but for many children with disabilities, this skill is not learned until later in life. Reach out to your school or childcare administration and ask them what initiatives and programs they have in place or will be building in the future to ensure inclusivity.

We understand that for many childcare centers the main barrier to inclusive centers comes back to funding and appropriate teacher-to-student ratios based on the children's abilities and needs. Even if centers wanted to support more families with disabilities, they are not able to without putting the cost on families. One way we can all advocate for inclusivity is to reach out to local legislatures and politicians and request subsidized funding for centers that support inclusive classrooms.

Whether you are currently part of a center that offers childcare, a fellow parent or an employer who has parents in their workforce, we can all agree that every child and parent deserves high-quality childcare. Together we can set an example and raise the bar for what it means to provide excellent childcare in our communities.

CHAPTER 4

UNWAVERING INTEGRITY

"With integrity, nothing else counts.
Without integrity, nothing else counts."

—WINSTON CHURCHILL

There is a recurring theme you are probably starting to pick up on as we share one story after the other, when families come to KOTM, it's not because everything in their world is going according to plan. Whether they knew their child would be born with a disability or are managing a recent diagnosis, and everything in between, many families come to us facing unimaginable sadness and grief, all while managing a mighty transition. In these incredibly vulnerable moments, these families need a trusted partner, someone who will come alongside them, assure them it's going to be OK, and do so with the utmost integrity.

Some of the most vulnerable families that we work with are those who take part in our Early Head Start program. While some of these families do have children with a disability, all of them come to us facing the challenges that come with living with low income or below the poverty line.

Alicia Lopez and her son Luis came to us with not just a need for a service, but for comprehensive support. As the sole provider for her son and a new mom, Alicia struggled to understand what was wrong with her son. Like many children born during the pandemic, he had not received much exposure in his little life to the outside world. But as COVID restrictions began to lift, and they attempted to get involved with other children and activities, Luis did not seem to engage like other children. Alicia unpacked her thinking at the time, "I just thought maybe COVID was the reason why when we started getting together with other kids, he would be off on his own, or maybe because he's used to being at home. At home, if he wants to run around, I can let him run around. If he wants to play outside, I'll let him go and play. So maybe he's not used to a regimen. I thought maybe he's just not used to it."

Alicia and Luis Lopez

Alicia attributed much of his behavior to needing more time to connect with other toddlers and experience the world around him. Additionally, Alicia could tell her son was developing slower than the typical noted milestones. So when she applied to the WIC program (a supplemental nutrition program for women, infants, and children), she asked the team there if they knew of any resources to help her son. Since little Luis was only eighteen months old, they referred her to KOTM for our early intervention program. She enrolled Luis in early intervention, but it was clear to the staff that she needed more support. Registering Luis was only one step, but the first step of a journey with KOTM that would transform their lives for the better.

The staff in early intervention could see that Alicia needed more support and helped her enroll in Early Head Start (EHS) through KOTM. EHS is a government-funded program rooted in equity, supporting children from the most at-risk backgrounds. Through a comprehensive model of support for the whole child and the whole family, EHS serves as a buffer to prevent and address childhood trauma, hunger, poor health, and other outcomes associated with living in poverty. EHS combines services such as education, early childhood development, health, nutrition, mental health, disability services, family support, and parental involvement to enhance the child's life and build a solid family unit.

Alicia's low income, lack of support and resources, and growing understanding of Luis's special needs made their family the perfect candidate for EHS where she could access comprehensive services that could benefit every area of their life.

Alicia, like the Killens and many other families, was no stranger to the stress and anxiety that comes with looking for quality and affordable childcare. Alicia explained, "You always hear these stories where the child gets neglected, or the teachers are too worried about other kids and don't really have time to pay attention to everyone, especially with daycare programs."

It was clear Luis's speech was delayed, and paired with the fact that he did not act like the other children, he would often choose to isolate himself. Alicia worried teachers would overlook Luis and shared her concerns, "I'm a single mom; how will I afford daycare? I could either take care of him, or I can go to work."

Thankfully, within the EHS program, the childcare is covered for her through age three, which was not only an answer to prayer but a game-changer for Alicia. Immediately, Alicia could see the difference in the quality of care offered. "When I came here, I saw how KOTM makes sure that there are enough teachers in the classroom to fully take care of the individual needs of each kid. Each kid is different. And seeing his teachers, like Alfa, pay special attention and even recognized things in Luis that I, as the parent, could not see."

Access to this kind of childcare was more than meeting a need for Alicia; it was liberating. Alicia explained, "He can be here all day, and I work and provide for him. It's extremely helpful not to have to worry about the bill coming in every month, and stress because I don't know how to pay for it."

For families like the Lopezes, the high cost of childcare creates a cycle of poverty that many become trapped in. You need childcare so you can work, but what is a family supposed to do if your job doesn't pay enough to cover childcare? Let alone having the ability to pursue education and employment opportunities to improve their circumstances and skills. Despite wanting the best for their children, many low-income families must explore options outside the quality of care their children deserve in order to find something within their budget. But at KOTM, through the EHS program, we can provide these families with both. They can go to work with peace of mind that their child is safe and having a great time in a caring and clean environment, surrounded by staff who are willing and excited to meet their unique needs.

TEAM LOPEZ

Alicia was no longer the only one looking out for Luis and trying to ensure he was hitting his milestones. They now had a team cheering them on and supporting them. Each of Luis's teachers was incredibly experienced; they deeply understood what is typical and when to raise a flag of concern. For example, they can easily spot the difference between a child having a hard time the first time they're separating from their mom versus when they should be comfortable by now, allowing them to point parents in the right direction.

Alicia shared, "We discovered Luis had some eyesight issues. The teachers noticed it before I did because they paid so much attention to him! They would see him put his face up close to items or pictures and often squint."

Alicia had a safe, judgment-free space to share her concerns about her son's development—something every parent needs, especially single parents who don't have a partner at home to process or help keep an eye on progress. As a mother of six with a supportive husband, family, and community, I know what it's like to wonder if your kid is just being a kid or if you're seeing a sign of a more significant issue. Often, nothing is scarier for a parent.

Alicia had always noticed that her son's behavior and reactions differed from other children's. She would compare Luis to his cousins or her friends' children and feel immense guilt, believing she was the cause of his behavior. When other children were told "no," they may become upset but would move on. But, when Luis was told no, he would completely melt down for extended periods.

In fact, any time they left the house, Luis would cry practically non-stop. Alicia would ask herself, "What am I doing wrong as a mother that my child can't go to stores without starting to cry?" His crying was so stressful for Alicia that she would leave the house as little as possible. "As a single mom, you want to socialize and ensure your child has friends. You want to have friends, gather with people you care about, and just build a community. When you can't do that, it's really lonely and really hard."

Instead of taking him to run errands, Alicia would try to find someone to watch him and return as quickly as possible; otherwise, he would scream non-stop. If she did have to take him into the store, she would go in for the bare minimum items they needed, keeping any shopping trip to ten minutes max.

When she shared all of this with Luis's EHS teachers, they gave her signs to watch out for at home. For example, tantrums shouldn't last any longer than a minute or two, and she should be on the lookout for aggression that is outside the norm of what you see in a toddler his age.

Eventually, the teachers and the EHS team began to recognize some of the telltale signs of autism. They recommended that Luis see a physician and have the preliminary tests done. Alicia explained, "They gave me resources to help him, not just telling me 'You need to help him' and then leaving me on my own to somehow figure it out." The EHS staff came alongside her every step of the way, ensuring she knew what steps to take next and where to go.

After seeing multiple healthcare professionals and having completed the necessary testing, the results were in: Luis did have ASD. Yet again, through the Early Head Start program, our team rallied around her to quickly get him the support he needed.

When individuals face life-altering challenges such as disabilities, financial struggles, or other unforeseen circumstances, there's often a common belief that a single program, a visit to a specific doctor, or even a particular medication could serve as a cure-all. However, the reality is more complex; there's no one-size-fits-all solution. Like the Lopez family, vulnerable families usually require access to a range of supportive services rather than relying on a singular remedy.

Comprehensive care extends beyond the child's health, encompassing the well-being of the caregiver or parent. Our Respite Care program proved to also be a lifeline for Alicia, affording her a much-needed break to replenish her own well-being, ensuring she has the capacity to care for Luis. Alicia expressed, "Respite has given me that breather that I need. As a single mom, I don't really have my parents, so if I want to go out, I can't just call my mom and say, 'Hey, come pick up my kid.' Or 'Do you want to see your grandchild?' Also, because of his autism, he doesn't do well with strangers—it limits options. But with respite, it's in the evening from six to nine o'clock. That gives me time to have adult time, go to dinner with just adults, and talk about adult issues without worrying. Is he doing OK? Is he crying? Can the babysitter handle him?"

Alicia's eyes welled with tears as she continued, "With respite, they're just so great with him, and they know that he has these needs, and they are able to work with it."

Hear Alicia's Story of Transformation: Learn How Comprehensive Support and Unyielding Love for Luis Altered Their Lives.

chasingtheimpossiblebook.com/chapter4

I cannot express enough my gratitude for Alicia's courage in sharing her story. For many vulnerable families like Alicia, their situations are nuanced. Through KOTM, Alicia accessed early intervention services, enrolled in EHS, as well as other programs, and utilized respite care. When individuals require comprehensive resources, it's easy for them to be overlooked or slip through the cracks. That's why integrity is crucial to our approach to care.

Operating with integrity goes beyond enrolling someone in a program, checking off boxes, and sending them on their way. It involves rolling up our sleeves and becoming deeply involved. It means every family has a partner in their child's teacher. Every employee approaches our families with a "what do you need" rather than a "here you go" mindset. We are honest about what the child truly needs. Often this includes providing unfunded visits to ensure the child has the necessary resources. Integrity means going above and beyond to create a supportive work environment building up our staff for the long term. It also means listening to parents and adding programs and services to help meet the parent, child, and family needs.

Is it easy? No. But it's what our integrity demands. And the results show that this radical approach works.

Time and again, families graduate from our services and programs full of hope. Alicia is one of those parents. She shared, "It took Luis three years to learn to say 'mom,' and at one point, I thought he wasn't ever going to say it. So, when he finally did, I just literally cried. To hear him finally say it was amazing." She continued, "Being with KOTM, I realized that he can still have big dreams. It'll just be a little bit different. It may not be the easiest way to achieve them, but he will be able to. There's still hope. He can still live a great life."

A KIDS ON THE MOVE MOMENT

Barbara Quintana, Eligibility, Recruitment, Selection, Enrollment, and Attendance (ERSEA) Manager

My name is Barbara Quintana, and I joined the staff at KOTM thirteen years ago. My husband and I moved to Utah twenty-six years ago from a small town just outside of Mexico City. Our children, Brenda and Daniel, were little, and being foreign, it was a challenge. Someone told me about the Head Start program and suggested that it would be a good opportunity for my family.

When we joined the program, I was excited to see the classrooms and the different areas they assigned for playing, relaxing, and more. I was able to observe the routine the kids had in the classroom, and we were encouraged to get involved with the program in different ways. I would volunteer in the classroom, helping the teacher and reading books to the children. Coming here as an immigrant, I didn't know anyone. I only knew my husband and my kids, and that was it. So this was also a good opportunity to get to know other families with children the same age.

The Head Start program also gave us activities we could do with our kids in the home. For example, they gave us a list of activities that anyone can do in their home with their kids, using what you already have in the house. When you are a low-income family, you don't have the money to buy all the toys or latest activities. You have to use the same materials that you would already have in the house. The activities would help us teach our children how to use pictures around the house to spot colors, shapes, items that match, and more.

Head Start also taught me how to provide a healthy and safe environment in our home. From covering electrical outlets to how to properly store chemicals and referrals for medical and mental health services. We would receive reminders to take the kids to the doctors, and they would receive well-check exams and dental exams. My family would not have had the opportunity to access these resources were it not for Head Start.

When we lived in Mexico, I had earned a law degree, but when we moved here, my first challenge was to learn English. Head Start was able to provide me with the opportunity to take college classes where I could learn English. Once I learned English, I took classes online at the University of Cincinnati in early education. I earned a new degree in the States; luckily, they accepted some of my credits from Mexico, and I became a kindergarten teacher.

When it was time for my kids to transition out of Head Start, we created a plan and defined what elements my children would need. We had the opportunity to speak with other families, find out what schools their kids were going to, and ask questions on how to enroll.

I saw the positive impacts that Head Start had on my children. Growing up, they both loved to read and now they are both in school full-time. My daughter, Brenda, is pursuing a master's in labor studies, and my son is studying business.

I'll never forget when I learned that KOTM was expanding and hiring new staff. I was so excited to apply. As a parent, I had such a great experience, and KOTM had a fantastic reputation for being a wonderful place to work. When I received the news that I was hired...Oh my gosh, I was so happy. I still remember my first day; there were eleven of us family educators being brought on and starting our training. After three months of studying and hard work, I was evaluated and passed.

We all want the best for our children and to give them a chance to grow up happy and healthy, and for the past thirteen years, I have felt so proud to open the same doors to resources and opportunities that were provided to my family. I often work with Hispanic families who are facing the same challenges that we once did. Answering the questions, tracking down answers, and building a relationship during my home visit. With my education, I am able to explain to these families how the brain works and how important those first few years are for their child's brain development. If they provide good, positive experiences, they are going to create an impact that their child will benefit from for the rest of their lives.

BRINGING EARLY HEAD START AND THE HEAD START PROGRAM TO KIDS ON THE MOVE

Yes, KOTM was founded originally with the goal of helping kids and families with Down syndrome, but the heart behind it was always to help the most vulnerable members of our community. Karen and Brenda never wanted to limit resources to a specific group of people.

Children from lower-income homes are at a higher risk of neglect and are more likely to experience food and housing insecurity. We see the impact in their behavior and academics, as many of these children struggle to keep up with their peers in school.[10] And for the low-income families also navigating their circumstances with a child with disabilities, as you can imagine, the stakes are even higher. According to the National Library of Medicine, children who grow up in poverty are less likely to be treated for their conditions, as they generally have more limited access to care, and even those with insurance may face additional barriers and consequently have poorer health outcomes.[11]

Law associated with the Head Start program mandates that 10 percent of these resources are set aside for children with disabilities.[12] So for Karen and Brenda, the decision to apply to become an Early Head Start provider was an easy one. If there was something that they could do to help, and the government was making it possible, they wanted in.

Early Head Start helps hundreds of thousands of vulnerable families every year in the United States. From 2021 to 2022, throughout the year, a total of 214,300 infants and toddlers and 12,552 pregnant women participated in Early Head Start. Of these 214,300 children served, 18,156 experienced homelessness, 10,189 were in foster care, and 27,410 had a diagnosed disability.[13]

In theory, as a culture, we understand that growing up in poverty or low income can be detrimental. But also, as Americans, we have a

---

10   The United Way, "Child poverty in America – facts, statistics | United Way NCA," United Way of the National Capital Area, October 26, 2022, accessed November 9, 2023, https://unitedwaynca.org/blog/child-poverty-in-america/.

11   National Library of Medicine, "Poverty and childhood disability – mental disorders and disabilities among low-income children," NCBI, accessed November 9, 2023, https://www.ncbi.nlm.nih.gov/books/NBK332898/.

12   U.S. Department of Health and Human Services, Administration for Children and Families, Office of Head Start. "What to Know About the 10% Eligibility Requirement." Early Childhood Learning & Knowledge Center (ECLKC), 20 Mar. 2024, https://eclkc.ohs.acf.hhs.gov/publication/what-know-about-10-eligibility-requirement.

13   National Head Start Association, "Early head Ssart facts & figures – NHSA," National Head Start Association, accessed November 9, 2023, https://nhsa.org/resource/early-head-start-facts-figures/.

can-do attitude. We believe that anyone who truly wants to succeed, can. And while technically, that is true, it's not the whole truth. The stats show it's not as simple as picking yourself up by your bootstraps. Children who grow up poor are more likely to be poor as adults. While roughly 37 percent of children who were never poor completed college by age twenty-five, only 3 percent of children from persistently poor backgrounds could do the same. The study found that poverty played a role, even when race, gender, parents' education, and other factors were taken into account. Research shows that children who grow up in poverty are also more likely to develop chronic illnesses such as asthma or obesity—the latter can lead to further health problems, including diabetes and heart disease. And we all know that medical debt is the fastest way to accumulate debt in this country.

Having been raised in a low income and abusive household, and left to provide for myself at only sixteen, I am one of those people who picked myself up by my bootstraps. As a speaker and thought leader, I encourage people every single day to take accountability for their lives and find a way to move their lives forward.

But I can also recognize that two things can be true at the same time, and statistically I was an anomaly. It is incredibly rare, practically impossible, for someone with so many obstacles, and with no support or community, to create a life that looks like mine. And because of that, I am an advocate for expanding access to programs like EHS and Head Start. Because while I was able to make it on my own, as a resident of one of the most technologically advanced and economically advantaged countries in the world, a country that gives over $39 billion in foreign aid each year, I also believe that there is no reason why anyone should have to go it alone.[14] So today I choose to be the kind of person I wish had been there when I was in need of help, fighting to ensure the Alicias and Luises of the world would have a path forward and have at least some small chance at a good life.

Saying anyone who wants to escape poverty can is like saying anyone who wants to climb Mt. Everest can. If you want to climb Mt. Everest, it takes an immense amount of resources and training. If you want to escape a life of poverty, it takes education, access to resources, and a support system. Early Head Start and Head Start provide that for families, giving them a fighting chance for the grueling climb.

Despite this amazing resource being available both to families with and without children with disabilities and the large number of people who are taking advantage, only 10 percent of the people who qualify for Head Start actually have access to it.[15] This is in part due to lack of knowledge that the program exists or what it offers, but this is also partially because there are not enough organizations like KOTM who offer the program to meet the demand of their communities.

We are doing everything we can to address limited funding and these issues. We go and seek out communities we know are in need, from low-income clinics, struggling schools, places of worship, and other non-profit organizations; we go out into the communities and seek out the people who need this program. We are taking a proactive approach to try to find these families, many of whom wouldn't even know where to look.

---

14   George Ingram, "What every American should know about US foreign aid," *Brookings.Edu*, October 2, 2019, accessed January 18, 2024, www.brookings.edu/articles/what-every-american-should-know-about-u-s-foreign-aid/.

15   National Head Start Association, "Early head start facts & figures," October 2, 2019, accessed November 9, 2023, https://nhsa.org/, https://nhsa.org/resource/early-head-start-facts-figures/.

At KOTM, we keep a waitlist of people in the community whom we are not able to serve right away. This way, we can accurately reflect what the need is in the community. If we never show what the need is, we can't get the funding. Here in Utah, we are receiving more and more immigrants and refugees looking to start the next chapter of their lives. It's incredibly difficult to move to a new country, and then you layer on top of it the steep learning curve that comes with trying to understand a new educational and medical system: the barrier to finding resources can feel overwhelming. This is why we hire a very diverse workforce that can speak different languages.

Poverty spans generations within a family. Just like a family can pass down skills or knowledge, the opposite is also true, and you can pass down a lack of skill or knowledge. If your mom never took you to the dentist, you probably won't take your child to the dentist. One of the highest risk factors for being incarcerated is having a parent who was incarcerated.

Early Head Start gives these incredibly vulnerable families the highest opportunity for success. We have to help. We cannot turn our backs and say, that's not our problem.

A LOOK INSIDE EARLY HEAD START & HEAD START

Early Head Start works with expecting parents through the birth and until the child turns three, while Head Start provides services to families and children from three to five. They encourage both the development of the child and the parent, teaching the parent how to create a healthy attachment between them and their child. The services include prenatal health; medical, dental, and mental health for children and families; healthy meals and snacks; parent involvement opportunities; support for children with disabilities; and individualized education and services to children in need.

Head Start programs provide comprehensive services to enrolled children and their families, which include health, nutrition, social, and other services determined to be necessary by family needs assessments, in addition to education and cognitive development services. Head Start services are specifically designed to be responsive to each child and family's ethnic, cultural, and linguistic heritage.

Parents are encouraged to be actively involved in the program, as it empowers them to be their child's first teacher and advocate. This is something I hope we all can appreciate. At KOTM, we work with children who have complex diagnoses, and so often, we meet parents who were in denial or struggling to know how to help their child. When we are able to reach a child and the parent is able to see improvement and take an active part in helping the child succeed, it's much more meaningful. The importance of a parent's role in their child's development cannot be overstated.

This incredible resource does not just teach a child from a disadvantaged background to thrive but also puts the entire family on the road to success. In fact, research indicates that the children who participated in Early Head Start and Head Start had better academic, social, and emotional skills at ages two, three, and four than those who did not receive any services.

Even though KOTM began with a mission to help children with Down syndrome, that has not stopped us from constantly looking for the next need and then figuring out how to meet it. The founders, Karen and Brenda, knew that every child is precious and worth fighting for, and we have never strayed from that mission

Families can access our programs by going to our website or calling in, and being connected with our Intake Coordinator or

ERSEA (Eligibility, Recruitment, Selection, Enrollment, and Attendance) Manager to complete an application and interview. We maintain a waitlist so if we are not able to help right away, we can get the resources to those families as soon as possible. When an opening becomes available in the program, we will reach out to those families to inform them of openings.

Unfortunately, it is at this point in the enrollment process where we see the most drop-off; the family has to commit to coming in for the appointments, and they may be hesitant to do that. For the most part, our staff are able to get the family enrolled and help them understand the amazing opportunities that are available to them, which helps to mitigate any fears or concerns that the family might have. After that, the family is able to fully enroll and take advantage of the services that we have to offer.

For Alicia and so many other families in Utah, KOTM has been that partner they needed. Our Early Head Start program has become a lifeline for them. Alicia said it best, "Sometimes when you're in a hard place, all you see is darkness. With KOTM, I saw the light. It's been an amazing journey, and it's not over yet."

This is not a one-and-done program. We are in this with families for the long haul. We are committed to helping families and all the children like Luis to continue to thrive and succeed in their lives. Through Early Head Start, and hopefully one day Head Start, we are transforming lives, creating a ripple effect in our community, and proving that with compassion and integrity, anything is possible.

YOUR MOVE
Build a Future Together

Currently, there's only one other Early Head Start provider in Utah County, and they can only accommodate sixteen children at a time. In a region with a population of 700,000, our current capacity stands at just 152 slots. The need is vast, and so are the aspirations to do more. We're reaching out to you, our incredible community, because we need your support to expand our classrooms and continue advocating for families in need.

The truth is, we want to do more, and we can! Currently we only have an Early Head Start program for children ages birth to three years old; afterward we refer out to a Head Start provider which services ages three to five. We would love to expand and offer an age three- to five-year Head Start program so that families can stay with KOTM. This requires a larger facility with more classrooms and doubling our capacity so all children could continue to age five and apply for Head Start funding. A new facility would bring us one step closer.

By securing additional funding, we aim to proactively build more classrooms, making space for more children and their families. With your help, we can obtain the facilities we need, enabling us to bid for grants that will significantly increase our program's reach. Imagine the positive impact we can create when given the chance to serve more vulnerable families and children!

Now, here's where it gets exciting. Our new building fund isn't just about classrooms; it's about securing 20 acres of space. Initially, we thought it was for the future, but after working closely with architects, we realize half these acres are necessary today to meet the urgent needs of our community. We're looking to the future, and we're ready to build it now.

 Explore Our Vision for the Future: Delve into the 3D Blueprint of Our Revolutionary Campus and Discover How Your Contribution Can Shape the Landscape of Comprehensive Care.

kotm.org/strategic-initiative

And here's where you come in—we need your help to make this vision a reality. Our community rallied around us nearly forty years ago, from donated land, architectural drawings, monetary donations, physical materials such as concrete and wood, to various trade groups donating their time, craftsmanship, and labor to construct the building we have today. As we look forward to the next forty years, we are calling on each of you to help us do it again. By supporting KOTM, you're not just contributing to a program; you're building futures, offering opportunities, and creating a ripple effect of positive change in our community.

Yes, the needs of our community are significant. Yes, it's a challenge. But challenges are opportunities for growth, and that's where we need to step in. A rising tide lifts all boats, and together, we can be that tide. In a world that often emphasizes self-reliance over community support, we're choosing a different path—one that welcomes everyone, regardless of their circumstances. We believe everyone is worthy of a bright future, and we're on a journey to ensure everyone has an opportunity to have their needs met.

Operating with integrity is our foundation. As Brené Brown so eloquently put it, "Integrity is choosing courage over comfort; it's choosing what's right over what's fun, fast, or easy; and it's practicing your values, not just professing them."[16] Karen and Brenda, the visionaries behind KOTM, have consistently chosen courage and compassion over what may have seemed easier. Some would say, and many did, that what they were trying to accomplish was impossible, yet they did it. In a world that can sometimes be divisive, we are here to unite and create positive change.

So, let's debunk the myth of easy answers. Supporting vulnerable families is not about the simplicity of hard work; it's about standing together, embracing the courage to make a difference, and creating lasting change. Will you join us on this journey to make the impossible possible once again?

As we embark on this mission, let's remember: Every child, every family, and every supporter makes a difference. Let's build futures together.

---

16   Brené Brown, *Dare to Lead* (London: Vermilion, 2018).

CHAPTER 5

EXPERT CARE FOR LONG-TERM SUCCESS

"I really think that a little bit of change can really have a huge impact."

—AUBREY ZARUBA, KOTM EMPLOYEE

Kendyl and Brandon Madsen were over the moon after discovering they were expecting their second child. After months of grueling IVF treatments, the emotional and physical roller coaster was worth it. They had endured countless shots, tests, and procedures, and their joy knew no bounds when the procedure to implant an embryo, which they knew would be a little girl, was a success. The world was their oyster as they began to imagine their family of four, with their son Maddox being the best big brother. Kendyl's pregnancy seemed to be going as planned when they went in for their fifteen-week anatomy scan.

Yet, at that crucial pre-natal check, their world was turned upside down when they learned that their daughter, Monroe, had hydrocephalus. Kendyl recalls, "We found out at a 15-week scan that she had enlarged ventricles, and we'd need to meet with a maternal-fetal medicine specialist." Suddenly, their vision of a future, watching their daughter say her first words and take her first steps, crumbled. So much of their new life was unknown, but one thing was certain: Monroe would have to overcome numerous obstacles to achieve what comes naturally to other children.

Kendyl and Brandon each processed the news in their own way. For Kendyl, as she pondered what life with a child with hydrocephalus could look like, she determined that she was going to love this child no matter what. For Brandon, he dived into researching the condition, trying his best to understand the intricacies and challenges his daughter would face. As they began meeting with doctors and specialists, one thing became clear: early intervention would be key to Monroe's growth.

Doctors explained that each child with hydrocephalus is like a "snowflake." No two children with the condition are the same in terms of their abilities or how the condition presents itself. Symptoms can vary significantly from person to person due to the buildup of cerebrospinal fluid in the brain's deep cavities. This meant the Madsens would not have a clear understanding of what lay ahead until after Monroe was born, including whether or not their little one would survive after delivery.

Kendyl shared, "We didn't know if she'd be able to breathe on her own. We didn't know if she'd be able to eat on her own. We didn't know if she would live through the delivery." The morning of their scheduled C-section, Brandon and Kendyl braced themselves. And when they heard their little girl cry on the other side of the cover, a wave of relief and joy washed over them. It was the best sound in the world.

In advance of her birth, they had been given every referral and resource they could potentially need. After they brought Monroe home from the NICU, the Madsens immediately got to work. Kendyl recounted, "Just knowing that we had a plan and resources from day one forward gave me a lot of peace and comfort." The couple understood that early intervention services would be critical. "They had been able to explain to me how early these services could actually start and that they would all be in our home to make things easier for me and for Monroe, to make us comfortable," Kendyl explained.

She went on to share, "But I had no idea of the number of services needed, how expansive it was for these kids. Thankfully, we have been able to take advantage of so many of the services needed through KOTM." Because we have so many types of therapies and services within our various programs at KOTM, almost everything the Madsens could potentially need to treat their daughter's complex condition was at their fingertips. From programs at the center to services that could come to their home, every therapy and treatment Monroe needed was easily accessible.

Kendyl described the power of having access to therapies in their home: "It was so hands-on and in our environment that it was a significantly better situation than maybe going to a clinic for a physical therapy appointment, which we've done before, and they've been phenomenal in their own way. But for her to be in her environment where she's obviously the most comfortable and she's playing with the same things every day, for them to be able to coach me on simple things I could do to make something like playing with a toy more beneficial for my daughter was a game-changer."

As Monroe attended appointment after appointment and Kendyl and Brandon worked with her daily to implement the strategies at home, she slowly began to make progress. Despite the pain, frustration, and immense amount of work needed, Monroe began to hit her milestones. And when she did, for Brandon and Kendyl, it was the best feeling in the world.

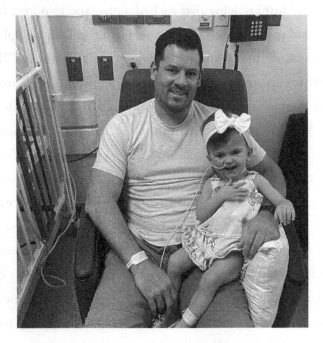

Brandon and Monroe Madsen

Kendyl recalled, "When she came to us, it was pretty scary. But then, to see her thrive has brought a unique amount of joy that I don't think I've ever felt before." But it was not just Monroe who was learning and growing. The whole family was transforming. Kendyl described the change with a smile spreading across her face and lighting up the entire room, "Seeing my husband, who's just so strong and stoic, just melt when his little girl's around—it's incredible. His compassion and empathy, and my compassion and empathy, have reached levels that I never felt before. And I am so grateful because it has also made me more compassionate and empathetic as I have watched all she has to do, all the hard work. She's had to go through all the pain, all the surgeries, all of the stuff we force her to do to make her life better. And when anyone else in our lives has something hard happen, we just kind of know how hard it feels and how much it hurts."

Discover Kendyl and Monroe's Uplifting Story: Experience the Radiance of Early Intervention in Bringing Joy and Transformation to Their Family.

chasingtheimpossiblebook.com/chapter5

UNDERSTANDING EARLY INTERVENTION

The Madsens' story is a testament to the power of early intervention in helping children with complex medical conditions. Just as early intervention services are vital for children on the autism spectrum, they play a crucial role in the development of children facing a range of developmental challenges.

Early Intervention (EI) is the process of providing therapeutic and support services to children who may have developmental delays or disabilities, as well as their families. These services can include speech therapy, occupational therapy, physical therapy, and more, tailored to each child's needs.

Every child is unique, and early intervention is a personalized approach. It starts with the creation of an Individualized Family Service Plan (IFSP), which outlines the goals for the child and family, as well as the services they will receive to help them reach those goals. The Early Intervention team works with the child and family to ensure the child's development is on the right track.

Early intervention programs recognize the significance of the early years, which we like to call the "sponge years." During these critical early years, children undergo rapid development, and the services and support they receive can profoundly impact their future.

For children like Monroe, early intervention services are invaluable. They not only help children develop the necessary skills but also provide them with a nurturing and supportive environment. These services are crucial in enabling children to thrive and reach their full potential, giving them the best possible start in life.

A KIDS ON THE MOVE MOMENT

Aubrey Zaruba, Development Specialist Leader

My name is Aubrey Zaruba, and I have been honored to, as of today, be a part of KOTM for the past twenty years. I had been working in ABA therapy for a year after college when I came to KOTM, and I have been here ever since.

KOTM has a really unique culture. From the very beginning, when Karen and Brenda started KOTM, they wanted it to be a place where people could come and feel comfortable with their children, and they created an atmosphere that was very family-friendly. In doing that, they created a company that also promoted a cultural experience for the employees where, yes, it's our job, but we also create a lot of really deep relationships both with the families that we work with and our coworkers. I don't live close to family, and I haven't since graduating college. I often think about the fact that I see these families I work with way more often than I see my own family. And I see my coworkers more often than I see most of my other friends.

It's really important that we work well together and support each other in our work responsibilities and endeavors. Because of the team atmosphere and the way the staffing is structured, it's kind of understood that we help each other. It's not really an option to be selfish here. Of course, you have to take care of yourself and your family, and there's space for that, but there's also just really an expectation that we take care of each other, too, while we take care of the families that we serve.

I think that's pretty unique, and I'm not sure how many places have that sort of culture. It's sort of a sense of family camaraderie.

We also take steps to ensure our teams have the mental and emotional support they need. As people deal with more and more emotional challenges and burnout, we do our best to have scheduled times to recharge, such as our early intervention staff retreat, or small things we do throughout the year, such as catering lunch for the staff, or gift certificates when our staff hit a goal. We even have a wellness committee that, for the past two years, focused on employee wellness. They will launch programs that focus on physical, mental, or emotional wellness. It's wonderful to have the support of the leadership to really make sure we are taking care of ourselves so we can take care of the families.

Recently, I was teaching floor time, and a mom stayed after class. As we chatted, she got a little emotional and asked, "I am just curious, how much time am I supposed to be doing this (referring to techniques we went over that evening) because I work full-time from home, I have the toddler and a baby. I'm also trying to keep the house clean and cook and all these things." She began to cry as she shared, "Sometimes I worry that she's delayed because I'm not doing enough." Which is very common; I think every mom feels that in whatever they've got going on.

So I took a moment to encourage her; I just said, "No, I don't want you to feel that way at all. I want you to know that a little bit goes a long way. What we're talking about is just making a few little tweaks with things that you're already doing with your daughter. You shouldn't feel like you need to be spending hours of time working on these things."

Whether it's intervention strategies, encouraging our staff, or being a listening ear for an overwhelmed mom, a little bit of kindness can go a long way. A little bit of patience can go a long way. Also, a little bit of your resources can go a long way to the community if you're feeling compelled to donate somewhere.

If every person we knew donated a dollar to KOTM, think of the impact that fundraising could have. We sometimes get overwhelmed by all the problems, whether it be the healthcare system, the education system, the economy, politics, the list goes on and on. We look at the enormousness of these problems and think there's no way we could make a difference, but truly, just the smallest bit of change can have a huge impact.

WHAT HAPPENS WHEN A CHILD FALLS THROUGH THE CRACKS?

As we have mentioned before, children experience incredibly large developments at a young age, their brains are creating foundational connections that they will use for the rest of their lives. It stands to reason that if they do not develop those foundational skills early on, it can impact the trajectory of their entire lives. For example, if a child didn't correctly develop their coordination in those toddler years, let's say they skipped crawling, they may struggle with coordination, which will look like difficulty holding a pencil. As they struggle to follow their teacher's direction, they may not understand why they aren't able to write like the other children.

While you and I understand that it's a motor skill that needs to be developed, children internalize their struggles—which often results in a negative belief system and frustration that manifests itself in their behavior. This was the exact case for one of my dearest friends, whom we'll call Elizabeth, and her son, whom we'll call LJ.

When LJ turned two, Elizabeth knew something was up, but she couldn't quite put her finger on it. Concerned, she spoke to his pediatrician. Since LJ was technically hitting his milestones, the pediatrician said Elizabeth shouldn't worry and sent them on their way. But Elizabeth's gut just kept telling her that something wasn't right. Elizabeth would look at the milestone checklist, and he was hitting them… but not really. For instance, when LJ played with other children, she noticed he was a little slower. Trying to do right by her son, she consulted three pediatricians, and each one said nothing was wrong, but Elizabeth continued to see the signs.

When he was two years old, LJ attended an in-home daycare, but his behavior was so challenging the provider told Elizabeth he was not a good fit. When he was three years old, he ran away from a preschool, which was located between two main roads. A woman, who happened to be a schoolteacher, found him and called the police. Looking back, Elizabeth can now see that LJ ran away because he was so incredibly frustrated with the teachers but did not have the words or abilities to communicate his feelings. When LJ would have an outburst, the teachers did not see a child struggling with big feelings; they just saw a kid who refused to behave. In a short period of time, her son was kicked out of three different preschools.

Around this time, Elizabeth enrolled him in a tumbling class, hoping it would help with his coordination. And while LJ would watch his instructor, he couldn't mimic their movements and would seem to get his limbs all mixed up. Looking back, Elizabeth realizes that this was one of the first clear signs of dyslexia, but neither the preschool nor the pediatrician could see it.

With kindergarten on the horizon, Elizabeth was worried LJ would not do well unless he had some sort of help. So, she enrolled him in the Stars Program, a medically run program at the University of Utah, and after three months of observation, testing, therapy, worksheets, and documentation, they finally received some answers.

He was diagnosed with ADHD and debilitating anxiety and prescribed Adderall and anxiety medication. Yet, once again, this pediatrician continued to insist LJ's problem was only behavioral (spoiler alert: it wasn't), and without a referral the insurance company attempted to deny their claim and almost didn't pay for LJ's needed medication. So, Elizabeth went back to the pediatrician and insisted he sign the referral in order to have the cost covered by insurance. Thankfully, the pediatrician agreed to sign but as he did, he insisted there was no issue, but if there was one his elementary school could flag it.

Unfortunately, Elizabeth would not find any support at his elementary school, as the staff flat-out refused to test LJ for dyslexia.

When it became clear that LJ was not keeping up with his classmates and needed an Individualized Education Plan (IEP), Elizabeth asked the psychologist from the University of Utah to attend and advocate on his behalf. Despite the presence of the community's esteemed medical professional and researcher, the school continued to deny testing for dyslexia. At this point, Elizabeth believed that their refusal was due to a reluctance to pay for the services.

Sweet LJ grew increasingly frustrated as he struggled to learn, which understandably increased his anxiety. The brain shuts off the learning process with debilitating anxiety, and he was distracted due to ADHD. All throughout 3rd and 4th grades, he would reverse words and refuse to write. His verbal vocabulary was above average, but in writing and reading, he was falling behind. All the while, the medical professionals kept declaring he would "grow out of it."

By 7th grade, LJ still wasn't writing legibly, so Elizabeth enrolled him in a local learning center that specializes in helping kids with learning disabilities. They gave LJ various activities designed to activate parts of his brain that had essentially switched off in the early years after not receiving the early intervention services he needed. LJ attended three times a week and had homework to complete every single day.

This was the moment everything changed; LJ's behavior, attitude, and attention transformed. The school eventually reported back to Elizabeth, "I don't know what you did, but he is a completely different person than last year." He was a different student, and he was ready to learn. Today, LJ is a senior in high school, on track to graduate, and doing so much better. His confidence has increased, and he bounces between a 2.9 and 3.0 GPA.

I've known LJ his entire life, and I knew nothing of his struggles until he was thirteen years old. He had written a congratulations card and tender note to my daughter. When I read it and saw his handwriting, I immediately knew he struggled. Later, I asked Elizabeth about his struggle, and she shared with me all that they had been facing. I am one of Elizabeth's closest friends, and for years, I never knew her son had any learning or behavior challenges. To me, he was just a kind, wonderful spirit, and friendly boy. Elizabeth hadn't opened up about their situation because she didn't think people would understand, not even her closest friends. After years and years of being gaslighted and ignored by medical professionals, I do not blame her. And while Elizabeth does wish that LJ's pediatrician had at least discussed early intervention services or other resources, like KOTM, with their family, who knows whether he was even aware of such services?

While I am incredibly thankful that LJ's story has a happy ending, the years of pain, fear, and frustration were completely avoidable. Thankfully my courageous friend Elizabeth listened to her intuition and continued to advocate for her son. But imagine the years of tears and frustration that their family could have been saved from if the school and pediatrician had truly listened to the concerns of a mother who knows her child better than anyone in the world.

When a child is missing milestones, or in LJ's case, only "sort of" hitting them, and they do not receive the necessary intervention, you set them on a dangerous path. Yes, like LJ, they may eventually catch up academically, but there is a bigger setback than just grades. The real danger lies when someone grows up believing they are incapable of learning.

Think about it, we have all had a negative experience that made us believe we were not good at something. Maybe it was a sport that you never excelled in, a new software that was not intuitive, or a subject you have always struggled to understand. What happened after a period of prolonged frustration? Chances are you gave up. This makes sense because, as we stated before, after a period of prolonged anxiety, the part of your brain that controls learning shuts down. The same happens when a child who never received the needed early intervention services experiences years of frustration.

For you or me, it's no big deal if we want to give up pickleball because we're not any good or decide to switch from a PC to a Mac because it's easier. But when a child decides to give up on learning because they think they are not smart, it sets them back for their entire lives. Thankfully, LJ's story has a happier ending, but there are probably thousands of LJs out there missing out on the help they need.

CATCHING THESE THINGS EARLY

My daughter, whom for this book I'll call Elsie, is our high-energy second-grader and has always been a force of nature. Whether it was at the dinner table or tackling her homework after school, we couldn't help but notice her wiggles and how she always ended up out of her chair. Like most parents, we encouraged her to stay seated but never thought much more of it. With her vibrant spirit and love for all things fun, we thought the need to move just came with the territory.

But when Elsie began to struggle with her schoolwork, we became concerned. Instead of completing a spelling test, Elsie had left the answers blank. Thankfully she has an amazing teacher who went the extra mile and gave her the test orally, which confirmed she knew the words. When I spoke to her at home about the blank test, Elsie explained, "There's so much going on around me, and I just forgot what the word was. I was frustrated because all the kids kept saying they were done, and I wasn't finished yet."

Little did we know, this behavior was just the tip of the iceberg. From memorizing phonograms to problems with other assignments, we could tell she was struggling. Trying to be proactive, we enrolled her in tutoring, but after two months of hard work, Elsie continued to struggle to keep up. At this point, we noticed Elsie was starting to internalize her struggle, saying, "I'm just not very smart." Or, "I guess I'm just not really good at spelling. I guess I'm not really good at math."

Of course, as her mom, I would do my best to reassure her, "No, honey, you are really smart. You are smart. We got through these words!" It was the negative self-talk that was a true red flag for me. I knew if we continued down this path, where my daughter is reinforcing this belief system that she can't learn, or she's not smart, or not as bright as the other kids, that it could derail her education. The last thing I wanted was for my daughter to develop a negative belief system about herself starting in second grade.

So, I began asking her some more specific questions about the classroom concerning her most recent spelling test, "Honey, when the teacher's saying the words and you're hearing everybody dropping their pencils and saying, 'I'm done!', are you just frustrated because they got done before you? Or are all the distractions causing you to lose your concentration? Is it like having ten televisions with the sound on all being played at the same time?"

Elsie immediately replied, "No, Mom, it's like a HUNDRED televisions at the same time." When she said that, it was like a lightbulb went off. No wonder she is having this problem. We made an appointment with our pediatrician, who luckily believed me and believed Elsie. She was diagnosed with ADHD, and we started her on a low dose of medication. We were lucky. The first medication we put her on completely worked. The very first day that she got the medication, she came home jumping up and down with joy, shouting, "Mom, I completed a hundred math facts in the five-minute timed test!" Starting a low dose of medication was a turning point.

Now, I'm not here to champion medication as a one-size-fits-all solution. What I do advocate for is giving children what they need. Each child is unique, and the solution varies. For Elsie, medication was the key. For LJ, it was specialized tutoring recognizing dyslexia, addressing the development of his motor skills, and opening his mind to different types of therapy. For Monroe, it was a symphony of early intervention services.

The Madsen family, LJ, and Elsie show us that intervening as soon as possible can make an incredible difference in the life of a child facing developmental challenges. The power of recognizing a child's needs and providing the right tools cannot be overstated.

No child should ever have to grow up feeling that they are incapable of learning. No child deserves to be treated as if their feelings of frustration are invalidated because they are not behaving the way an adult believes they should. No child runs away from a daycare where they feel heard, seen, and loved unless there is something deeper going on that needs to be addressed. No child leaves an answer to a spelling test completely blank because they want to get it wrong.

It should never be the responsibility of a child to convince the adults in their life that they need help. Rather, it is always the responsibility of the parents, teachers, doctors, and loved ones to see past what we consider "bad" behavior for what it truly is: a sign that a child is in need of help.

A KIDS ON THE MOVE MOMENT
Nathanael Sackett, KOTM Parent

When my wife, Dayla, was about twenty-seven weeks pregnant with our son, the doctors informed us that Jude had an extra chromosome and had Down syndrome. Initially, when we got the news, I was feeling a little sad and also worried for Jude. I understand, more than most, that life with Down syndrome can be a little bit harder and different in many ways, and the anticipation of the challenges ahead made me sad for my son.

You see, I have seventeen siblings; nine were adopted, and seven of my nine adopted siblings have disabilities. So, my mother was one of the first people we called after we spoke to the doctor. She, as you can imagine, is an amazing woman, and she understood deeply the sadness and worry we were walking through and validated our experience. But she also offered a lot of encouragement and hope. With

Down syndrome, you simply do not know what their natural abilities will be; some people with Down syndrome are nonverbal, while others are highly independent; they may work, drive, get married, and more.

Soon after receiving the news, we met with a genetic counselor. The counselor never asked us directly, but she did warn us that if we wanted to abort the pregnancy, the window when we would be able to do that was coming to a close. Without hesitation, we kindly let her know that we would not be terminating the pregnancy.

As a father and having grown up with siblings and relatives where someone with special needs is a part of your family, I'd say to anyone facing the decision to terminate a pregnancy: please don't.

In my family, we have seen a full spectrum of special needs: Down syndrome, autism, psychosis, three siblings with cerebral palsy, and DeGeorge syndrome, to name a few. There have been some truly challenging times that come with a disability, but I can say wholeheartedly that the benefits far outweigh the challenges.

My son, as well as each of my siblings with disabilities, has brought so many benefits to our family and the community. You invest in the relationships, in their success, and in them hitting those milestones just a bit more, and the whole process just makes you so thankful when they succeed.

We understand that there are very real challenges and valid reasons that would make raising a child with a disability difficult, for some, it's age, for others, an unsupportive community, difficult pregnancies and childbirth, and more; there is a lot of fear that comes with helping someone navigate life with a disability. I can understand that someone may not feel up for the challenge, but there are other options.

Nathanael, Dayla, AlleeJo, Ryan, and Jude Sackett

One of my sisters, due to her condition, literally only has one-third of her brain, as the other portion deteriorated when she was younger, and her head hasn't grown. The doctors counseled my family that she would die before she was four months old and definitely would not live past four years old. Today, she is in her twenties, and despite her condition, she walks, talks, and is brilliant. I really attribute this to the programs, like KOTM, that she had access to and the unconditional love and support of her family.

Jude and anyone with Down syndrome have very, very special roles in this world. Have you ever noticed how you feel and how you respond when someone with Down syndrome enters the room? You change, and you feel happier because they bring so much joy and love into every space they enter. No one else can do that.

Typically, in a room full of people, there's so much judgment and people serving their own interests. But people with Down syndrome simply love you, with no agenda, and that is pretty special. That's a pretty big gift that we all need. Please don't deny the world that gift.

A LITTLE INTERVENTION GOES A LONG WAY

Parenting in the twenty-first century brings its own brand of guilt, doesn't it? We find ourselves constantly critiquing every parenting decision. Am I spending enough time with my kids? Are they getting the right balance of foods? Should we be putting them in a music class? No matter what side of the country you live on, your political beliefs, or the size of your family, I can't think of one parent, especially mothers, who do not battle parental guilt.

Every single parent here at KOTM is no exception to this rule. The only difference is that their child's disabilities and struggles often compound their guilt. Not only do KOTM parents face the pressures of their personal life, professional life, managing the home, and the confines of modern parenthood, but there is the added pressure of attending therapy sessions, making up for lost time at school, spending time with their child practicing what they learned in therapy, and always wondering if what they are doing is going to be enough to ensure their child has their best chance at life.

The amount of therapy that a child could benefit from is probably endless. But with the demands of work, school, getting dinner on the table, and making sure their child is bathed and fed, it's simply not possible to fit everything into the day that could potentially benefit their child with disabilities. That is where our fantastic staff step in as a dedicated part of each child's support system.

Going back to our core belief that parent power is the biggest key to a child with a disability overcoming the impossible, we not only educate parents, but come alongside them as an emotional support. Laden with guilt, oftentimes, these parents ask, "Are we here because I didn't do enough at home or in those early days?" Or, "Are we practicing enough at home?" And just like our staff member Aubrey explained, we let them know that first and foremost, they are doing a great job, and second, we assure them that a little bit can go a long way. Parents are often so relieved when they understand that every waking moment doesn't have to be an extension of therapy. Oftentimes, just tweaking one small aspect of the playtime they already have with their children is more than enough to make an incredible difference. We really try to simplify the process for parents so that it easily folds into their schedule and how they live their lives.

By offering the educational and therapeutic support a child needs, with early intervention, we can help parents address issues before they snowball into a problem that can change the trajectory of a child's life. A small sign, such as a delay in a milestone or a behavior that signals that a connection was not made when they were little, can be corrected early on with minimal intervention. With my own daughter, we were able to identify her struggle while she was in second grade; for Kendyl, early intervention helped lay a strong foundation for the skills her daughter, Monroe, will need to tackle the challenges ahead.

Early Intervention is often the first step of a lifelong journey of providing care and support to a disabled child. Teal Kalt, another KOTM parent, learned shortly after delivery that her son Azure was born with Down syndrome. She enrolled him into our Early Intervention program when he was only four weeks old and participated in the program until he aged out at three years old. And while Azure has graduated from our Early Intervention program, the support they need as Azure grows has not diminished; in fact, it's one of their biggest challenges.

Teal shared with a look of frustration, "It's a challenge to try to make sure he gets all of his services, and he needs each of those services. The services are expensive if you were to try to access them privately. We have been forced to access them privately because most preschools/daycares have turned him away due to his disability. Of course, they can't legally say that because it's discriminatory. Instead, they have legal excuses that automatically disqualify him, 'Oh, he's four, he has to be potty trained' or 'Oh, we don't have enough staff to accommodate him.'"

Between the scheduling, the cost, and wanting Azure to have access to a classroom with typical children as well as needed therapies, the Kalt family has very few options. Teal went on to explain the toll it takes on her, "I feel guilty and ask myself often, should I quit my job? When daycare essentially costs the same as your salary, it's a hard choice to make. I want to keep working because I like my job, and I have my own things that I care about and goals. I don't know if I want to be a stay-at-home mom, but I also want to meet his needs. I struggle with a constant sense of tension: am I choosing myself over the things that would be best for Azure? And we only get one chance at him being four to five. What can we do to prepare him for kindergarten? And are we going to make the wrong choice?"

Teal and Azure Kalt

Teal's struggle is a common one. Many parents of children with disabilities have to make the heartbreaking choice between school and therapy, quality time as a family, versus more time in the car to get to appointments, hours at work to provide for their family, versus going without in order to manage the symphony of services their child needs.

This makes our need to expand our building and services all the more pressing. It's all well and good to look at numbers on a spreadsheet and see that there is a need. But here at KOTM, behind each of those numbers are the faces and stories of the families we love and cherish. We know that each day, they are fighting, hoping, and praying for a solution that can bridge the gaps in support and care they desperately need filled. We are working as fast and as hard as we can to expand and fill the gaps that threaten to swallow them whole each day.

YOUR MOVE
Parents, Trust Your Instincts

As the familiar saying goes, there is no instruction manual on how to be a parent. Whether your child is typically developing or has a disability, none of us was given a "how-to" manual despite how much we wished it existed. Sure, we can all look at the checklists of milestones that the hospital sends us home with, google things when we think it's an issue, and read relevant books. Yet, because each child is so unique, there simply is no "right way" to do this parenting thing. This is why I believe nothing, whether doctor, book, or "expert," trumps a parent's instincts or intuition.

With my own children when they were little, I always had a sixth sense when they had an ear infection, especially with my oldest. And every time I went to the doctor, I had a sinking feeling, knowing there was a chance that the doctor would think I was overreacting and tell me I shouldn't have brought them in. But of course, the doctors would confirm that my intuition had it right from the get-go.

My good friend Elizabeth *KNEW* that LJ needed support before anyone else did. You've already heard of almost half a dozen other stories of parents who knew something was off with their child. All of them did their best to petition and advocate to their pediatrician, schools, and other professionals for support, and yet only a fraction of them are believed and heard.

To every parent, I want to encourage you to trust your intuition regarding your child. Especially in those early days when the small voice inside of you is shouting, "Something is not right!" Despite

114

the fear that the doctor may not believe you, make the appointment. If they do not listen, get a second or third opinion. Track down the expert and have them seen without a referral if you have to.

Will it be uncomfortable? Absolutely. But your instincts will not steer you wrong.

CHAPTER 6

LIGHTENING THE LOAD

"You are beyond limitations and belong where infinite possibilities exist."

—HIRAL NAGDA

Anyone with children will tell you parenting is a full-time gig. The moment those soft, squishy newborns make their way into your arms, you become instantly consumed with their well-being. Driven by those parental instincts, every waking moment, especially the ones where you are supposed to be sleeping, is spent providing for their every need and making sure they are showered with love.

Yet, for many caregivers, parenting is not their only full-time gig. Many of us work full-time outside the home, have chores to accomplish, and a household to manage. And while healthcare professionals will advocate how important it is for parents to prioritize their self-care and make space for hobbies, fitness, or social life, it's easier said than done. The parents who are able to pull off creating space for themselves usually only do so in the slim margins of their lives.

When you layer in a child, or multiple children, with a disability, those slim margins for self-care disappear completely. The stakes are incredibly high when it comes to meeting the needs of a child with a disability. And unlike typically developing children, as children with disabilities age, they often do not gain the independence and autonomy that allow their parents more time to themselves. For our parents at KOTM, the opportunity to create a slim margin for self-care or to have a moment free of the demands of parenting can be a game-changer and elevate the quality of life of everyone in the home. This is certainly the case for the Benavidez family.

When little Ethan was only two years old, his mother, Morgan, could tell something was not quite right. Morgan recalled those early years: "He started to show a lot of aggression. And not even necessarily in response to being provoked, as if another child took his toy, and he responded by hitting, as happens with two-year-olds. Ethan, without any emotional or physical provocation at all, would just look at a kid and then hit him."

Morgan's husband, Marc, was also confused by Ethan's behavior. With plenty of nephews and nieces that he spent a lot of time with, he was pretty experienced when it came to children. But Ethan was a mystery to him. He shared, "My perception of things was that every child is different, but Ethan seemed very difficult to parent."

The couple did their best to try to communicate with Ethan and, when needed, discipline him in a way that was age-appropriate to let him know his aggressive behavior was not OK. "Whatever consequences or disciplines [we used] didn't work," Morgan went on, "nothing really seemed to click for him. Like, 'oh, I don't like this consequence, so I'm not going to do that again' with other kids. He didn't seem to learn from whatever parenting techniques I had at the time."

Eventually, Marc and Morgan welcomed a second son, Cruz, and finally, their youngest son, Mason, rounded out this little party of five. As Ethan grew, his parents expected he would grow out of this aggressive behavior, especially as his language skills developed, but nothing improved. Being the dedicated parents they are, the couple tried parenting classes, reading parenting books, and more, but to no avail. "As parents, we're trying to find the balance between showing our child kindness, love, and patience, but at the same time know his behavior is not ok and it has to be different," Marc explained.

As Ethan's behavior continued to escalate, the couple brought their concerns to several doctors and therapists, all of whom swept the parents' concerns under the rug. Morgan shared, "The first time that we went to a psychiatrist, Ethan was four; he basically told us that Ethan's too little. He suggested therapy but also said he may be too little to see a therapist, then wished us luck and sent us on our way. So, we got really no direction. When we went to check-ins with our pediatrician, I'd bring a list of concerns." Unfortunately, the pediatrician would issue another set of generic instructions, such as getting Ethan on a better schedule. Morgan continued, "Pediatricians do everything; they are not specialists in mental health."

Ethan was clearly struggling; he had huge emotional outbursts on a daily basis, but no matter where they turned or how hard they tried, Marc and Morgan couldn't get anyone to give them a straight answer. Then, one day, Ethan's words began to scare Morgan, "He started making comments about wanting to die and not wanting to live here anymore. 'That this isn't a happy place.' He was saying things that would be really heartbreaking to hear from anyone, of course, but from your four-year-old boy?" Morgan continued, "This was when I got really serious at the doctor's office. Demanding that they cannot just brush this off as an emotional little boy. He's clearly having a hard time."

After pushing and advocating, Morgan and Marc were finally able to get a doctor to diagnose Ethan. The result was depression and anxiety, and they started Ethan on medication. Shortly after visiting a psychiatrist, he was also diagnosed with Obsessive Compulsive Disorder (OCD) and Oppositional Defiance Disorder (ODD). While they knew the road ahead of them wasn't going to be easy, finally having a diagnosis meant they could at least understand how their son's brain was working, and how to support him. It was a game-changer. And so just a few years later, when their second son, Cruz, began showing similar signs, Morgan had him seen immediately. Like his brother, Cruz would eventually be diagnosed with anxiety and depression as well.

Ethan, Cruz, and Mason Benavidez

With two special needs sons, both in need of a high level of care, plus little Mason, the emotional, physical, and mental demands on Morgan and Marc were immense and unrelenting. Ethan's OCD meant he would often experience incredibly intrusive thoughts that made it difficult for him to function and even resulted in hallucinations. And since he was so young, it was incredibly difficult to coach and soothe Ethan when he was having one of his episodes. Morgan went on to explain, "He was having very, very distressing, obsessive thoughts, fears, or compulsions that don't necessarily even connect logically to the obsession. So, he'll have an obsession, such as thinking his mom is going to die in a car wreck. Then the compulsion might be, 'I have to flip the light switch four times when I come into the room.' It doesn't make any sense, and they don't have any control over the connection between the obsession and the compulsion. To have a little boy as young as he is trying to deal with that, that's really a lot."

As you can imagine, his condition also affected his behavior at school. Morgan went on, "I remember getting a message from the director saying they were having a hard time with Ethan. He keeps running out of the classroom, and he's telling staff that he's going to kill all the teachers. It caught us off guard, and while we all know that's coming from a four-year-old and not very credible, it's still kind of disturbing for him to even have those thoughts or to say those things to his preschool teachers."

Ethan did not "grow out" of his behaviors, and many of the adults in his life were unwilling to accept that they were not his fault. Morgan explained, "In second grade, he got in a lot of trouble for his tics from Tourette's and being disruptive in the classroom. The teacher just did not believe that he had Tourette's syndrome, despite the fact that we had a documented diagnosis from a medical professional."

Similar to his brother, Cruz was also four when symptoms of anxiety and depression began disrupting his life. This time, the signs were incredibly clear to Morgan: "He had totally withdrawn from his best friend and didn't want to play with her anymore. He didn't want to go to preschool. It was like he just totally changed almost overnight. He started to show these symptoms, and it lasted for weeks. Then, it would last for months. He's not eating, he's not playing; it was like we were watching his happiness and love of life slip away."

Once again, Morgan tried to bring Cruz's issues up to their pediatrician, and, once again, she was brushed off. The pediatrician suggested she could get him into counseling, which had a six-month waitlist, and that they would take a look again at his next well-child visit in a year. But Morgan was not having it, not this time around. Without a referral, she made an appointment with a psychiatrist who truly listened to her concerns, and Cruz was diagnosed that day with anxiety and depression. Having her concerns validated and addressed was an immense relief for Morgan, "I'm not just an overly concerned mother who's blowing things out of proportion. This really is concerning behavior. It was really, really a relief to get those diagnoses for Cruz, and he started an antidepressant right away."

While many people would be crushed under similar weight and demands, Marc and Morgan found a way for their family to not just survive but thrive. They were consistently in touch with their boys' care teams to assess the effectiveness of their medications and make adjustments as necessary. They partnered closely with their teachers to find ways to empower the boys academically and socially. And they continued to educate themselves and shift their parenting styles in a way that would work best for their boys.

Due to Ethan's oppositional defiance disorder, his natural instinct is to be combative and defiant during any moments of instruction or correction. In turn, it makes it incredibly difficult to help Ethan with even simple tasks, such as lacing up his rollerblades. But with patience and understanding, they still see small wins. Marc shared a recent win he had with Ethan: "Two weeks ago, Ethan finally let me teach him a different way to lace up shoes. We just took our time, and he struggled, but after about thirty minutes, Ethan shouted, 'I did it! I did it!'

I told him, 'That's awesome, man!'

He did it a few more times and continued to struggle. He finally looked at me and said, 'You know what? I find the other way a little bit easier, so I'm going to keep doing it that way.'

I replied, 'That's great, sounds good.' But I was excited that he actually let me help him learn a new skill, and that doesn't happen very often."

Morgan eventually decided to go back to school, and as part of her introduction to social work class, she was required to complete twenty hours of volunteer work. She discovered KOTM and decided to volunteer in our respite program. Respite Care is the temporary care of children with special needs, providing a short period of rest or relief to their usual caregivers. We provide the Respite Care program for children with special needs to give their families a three-hour break on weekend nights so caregivers can relieve stress, renew energy, and restore balance.

Morgan described her first experience with Respite Care, "I volunteered, and after the first couple of times, I realized it was not what I expected as far as volunteering with children with disabilities. I was imagining maybe these kids were deaf and blind or in a wheelchair or nonverbal or severely autistic and low functioning, but a lot of the kids here were not like that. They were kind of like *my* kids." Like many adults, due to the way our culture segments and stigmatizes those with a disability, Morgan had little exposure to children with disabilities, and until then, the dots hadn't connected that her sons were living day in and day out with a disability.

She went on to explain, "I kind of had that stereotype in my mind of what a child with disabilities is like. Then, after interacting with the families at KOTM, I realized, 'Wow! These families are like my family. We have these kids with diagnoses, problems, and struggles, and *WE* could benefit from this.' I got to see what the program is and was so impressed with all of the employees, the volunteers, the program, and the environment. Then I realized I could apply for this for my kids, and this could be really a blessing to them. And it has been!"

Dive Into the World of the Benavidez Family: Discover the Power of Support and How You Can Make a Lasting Difference in the Lives of Families in Need.

chasingtheimpossiblebook.com/chapter6

Now Ethan and Cruz come play at Respite Care on Friday, once a month, for three hours. And that three hours has been a lifeline for Marc and Morgan who, like every parent, need some time for themselves. The couple will often use the time to go on a date, sometimes accomplish an errand or chore with the ease that comes when you are child-free, or take the opportunity to shower their youngest, Mason, with undivided attention. The best part is Ethan and Cruz's love of coming to Respite Care, too, often counting down the days until their scheduled time.

And while Morgan and Marc are no strangers to calls from teachers about their kids, they often get a different type of phone call from the Respite Care volunteers. They gush about how much they love having Ethan and Cruz in the program and what amazing kids they are. As a parent, it is one of the most life-giving experiences when someone sees your child for the amazing person they are and truly values them. Respite Care is clearly more than just a break. It's a central source of mental, emotional, and physical support for every family that participates.

While I have met dozens of families in my time at KOTM, meeting the Benavidez family moved me to tears in a way I had not expected. These two young boys have an unseen disability that often means they live their lives being severely misunderstood and unfairly judged. It has moved me to ask what more we can do for parents of children with invisible disabilities. What resources or support can we provide to them so they have energy in the tank to continue caring and advocating for their child?

A KIDS ON THE MOVE MOMENT
Diane McNeill, Founder & Director of Respite Care

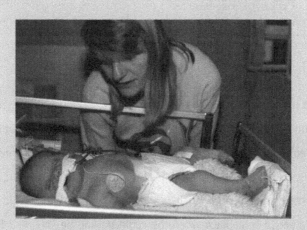

Diane and Brian McNeill

I'm Diane McNeill, and I'm currently the Respite Care Director here at KOTM. I'm also the founder of the program. My husband and I have three children, and our middle child, Brian, has Down syndrome.

Eventually, we would discover that he also has autism. He was also born with a club foot and intestinal blockage; Brian had nine surgeries before he turned six years old. During that time, I felt that, as a mother, I didn't have any support.

His first surgery was the same day he was born. Brian required a stay in the NICU, and at the time, I also had a fourteen-month-old at home. We managed it, but it was very stressful.

As he grew, it seemed we were always in the hospital or the emergency room for one reason or another, from whooping cough to follow-up and more. I couldn't help but become aware of other parents who were consistently at the hospital as well. As parents do, we started talking to each other, and we each felt like we didn't quite have the support we needed to address our individual situations. Each child with special needs is different, but the most important thing is to know whom you can ask questions and who understands so you don't feel alone. Keep in mind this was the early 1990s, and we didn't have the internet to help us research or find support groups.

I was experiencing this overwhelming sense of sadness like there was no end in sight. I started calling different places and asking what was available, only to discover that there were not any support services for parents of children with disabilities. At this point, Brian was ten, but he was still climbing pantry shelves and doing what a two-year-old would do. I needed someplace where he could go and be safe, and I could actually take a break, but there was nothing. Finally, I just sat down one day, and I found myself asking, "Is this what it's going to be like for the rest of my life?"

As I kept calling place after place, I finally connected with Kimber Dower, an occupational therapist. And she actually worked at a local hospital in the pediatric unit of occupational therapy. She saw the immense stress that the parents were under, and she had previously interned at a respite program. She told me on that call, "I've always wanted to start a respite program like the one I interned at."

I told her that I would help her get it started, and we just did it.

She would connect with people who came to the pediatric unit, saw the stress, and would ask if they wanted to be part of the respite care program. And they did! So, we started Friday's Kids Respite in 2000, and we hosted it every Friday night so the parents could go on a break.

Eventually, we connected with Karen and Brenda at KOTM, and they were incredibly supportive. They would let us use one classroom, and as our program grew, it expanded to two classrooms, three, and so on. Eventually, we merged with KOTM; I wanted to ensure that this program would be able to continue serving parents, even if one day I'm no longer able to be the one to manage it.

We developed our volunteer program in partnership with the local universities. The instructors have been excellent! They know how important it is for their students to get real-life experience in the field they are going into, so we have volunteers studying social work, pre-med, nursing, psychology, and more. It's just developed into a beautiful program where everybody is winning. We take the time to train each volunteer and let them know the importance of staying right with their child. We know not to even go an arm's length away. They must always be watching their child, keeping them right with you and making sure they're completely safe. They're at all different ages and all different levels. Some are putting things in their mouths, some are not, some are running, and some are making a straight line for the fire alarm. So, they have to stay right with their child, keep them safe, and redirect them if needed. But also, to have a ton of fun with them and let them experience the world to the best that we can safely. And they do.

As a result, the children have a safe, wonderful place to go. The parents get the break they need and feel at peace doing so, and these volunteers have experiences they never thought they would and really understand what it takes to care for children with special needs.

Many people do not understand that often special needs children need constant supervision, meaning day and night. When they're small, you're required to secure their room so they don't crawl out a window or sneak out of the house at night; sometimes, you have to switch the doorknobs where the lock is on the outside. You may lower a bed to the floor; some parents even sleep in the same room. These parents get little sleep, and then they get up in the morning and provide care all day long—preparing special diets, running them to appointments, and more, all while working and caring for their other children.

Right now, our Respite Care program supports eighty children, and we're hoping to increase that next year. For some of these families, the parents are the only ones who have ever cared for their special needs child before coming to Respite Care. To help everyone with the transition, we invite parents to come into the room and stay until their child is comfortable.

One mother began dropping off her two sons, both of whom had been diagnosed with autism. The first two times they attended, the boys would spend the first hour or so looking for their parents. But at their third visit, as their mom was signing them in, they headed straight for the classroom without even looking back to say goodbye. I'll never forget how that mother looked up at me with disbelief and shock on her face and said, "This is life-changing. I can't believe this is happening."

The fact that her boys felt so safe and secure meant everything. They understand that KOTM is a safe place where they can have fun; people are going to accept them and take care of them. It was such a rewarding moment for me, and it makes it all worth it to know that I've made a difference for a mom who was in the exact same place that I was in not long ago.

It's terrible to feel like you're alone, and the parents are just so grateful for time with their spouses and time with their other children. They can't believe that people would care about them enough to make sure that they have good lives and feel supported.

These children are amazing people, and at Respite Care, we love every single one of them. It's our honor to be able to be a part of their world and help them have the highest quality of life they can have.

A SIMPLE YET EFFECTIVE SOLUTION

Women like Diane are inspiring—cut from the same cloth as Karen and Brenda. Even though Diane was in the middle of her own challenges in raising her children and needing a break herself, she somehow had enough courage to dig deep beyond her own circumstances, her own suffering, and her own sadness and fatigue, and gave all that she had to lift another. She chased the impossible, creating something of significance out of nothing and changed the world for other children and families, leaving in her path a legacy of love, turning her pain into her passion and purpose.

I'll never forget the moment I realized the enormous impact that respite care has on families. It was 2014, and at that time, I was the COO. I headed out to my car one Friday evening and noticed the cars pulling into the parking lot filled with families dropping their kids off for Respite Care. Just a few rows over, I spotted a dad dressed in a suit and tie, and the mom was in a really lovely dress. They were clearly planning on a special evening.

The couple was talking to their son, who was about fourteen or fifteen, trying to gently coax him into the building. He was sitting on the ground, refusing to go in. I could hear them encouraging him, "Come on, buddy," and even trying to get him to move in the hopes of getting the momentum started. I figured this was their very first visit, as most kids, after they come once or twice, can't wait to come back.

I sat back for a moment to see how their conversation would unfold and how they were going to get him in the door. For about ten minutes, I watched from the front seat of my car as they begged, pleaded, and encouraged their son to go inside and give it a chance. I thought for sure if they could just get him in the door, he was going to be great!

A few more moments passed, and I was completely shocked as I watched the parents give each other that knowing look, and a wave of resignation washed over this poor couple. They then told their son they were all going home and quickly packed in the car and headed out.

I sat there stunned, with tears running down my cheeks, and my heart broke with the feeling of utter defeat that the couple must be experiencing on their drive home. You see, due to our limits in funding, volunteers, and space, we can only offer respite care to each family once a month. This means this was this couple's only shot at a date night for the whole month! And they would have to wait another month to try again.

If I had known then what I know now, I would have run inside to grab a staff member to assist. For the staff, it's a scene they are incredibly familiar with, and they have all kinds of strategies to get the kids excited enough about the evening or distracted enough so the parents can get out the door.

If you're a parent, you know that going out on a date isn't as simple as hiring a sitter and walking out the door. There are hours of preparation to get yourself and your kids ready for the evening. There is an entire process that has to happen that starts at two o'clock in the afternoon if childcare is going to come in at seven so you can go out for a couple of hours. The kids have to eat dinner, and you have to prep the house for the sitter. I mean, hello, you don't want the sitter to have to wade through a sea of dirty laundry in order to tuck your kids into bed. Moreover, any prep for the next day that you would normally do that evening has to be completed before you walk out the door. Then, on top of it, there is the planning, making reservations, and, finally, getting yourself ready.

All of the mental, emotional, and physical energy required for a night out when you have a typical child is compounded when you have a child with a disability. And the family I had watched from the parking lot, I'm sure, was no exception. They had probably spent all month looking forward to those three hours, and all day preparing for them. Thinking of them even now breaks my heart.

This need for respite care is not something we see just in the families we serve at KOTM but across the entire state of Utah. Diane McNeill, our Director of Respite Care, explains, "If you would want respite care services through the state of Utah's Division of Services for People with Disabilities, the first thing you have to do is get on the waiting list for respite services, and it can be years. I recently spoke with a family that had been on the list for fifteen and a half years, and they just recently were approved for services."

For children who require extensive, consistent support to meet both their physical and emotional needs, a parent may be with them practically 24/7. A parent may have paused their career in order to take care of their children and manage a symphony of treatments, therapy appointments, and educational needs. They are nurturing them, dressing them, feeding them, practicing what they learned in therapy, vigilantly keeping them safe, and showering them with love around the clock.

By offering respite care, we are empowering these families with a desperately needed resource that is incredibly scarce for families of children with disabilities. In doing so, we are giving parents the chance to be the best version of themselves so they can be the best parent for their child.

From day one, the purpose and vision behind KOTM has been to empower the parents so they have every opportunity needed to make sure their kids thrive and have a chance at a future. As our founder Brenda likes to say, we know the kids will be OK if the parents have what they need. Many times, that empowerment comes in the form of education; oftentimes, it comes in access to resources and professionals and an understanding of the community. And with our Respite Care program, that empowerment comes in the form of rest and time to recharge.

As Marc Benavidez shared, "Morgan's and our other families are far away. It's hard to try to find someone that we're comfortable leaving them with. Not because we don't trust them necessarily, but because their behaviors and their struggles are really challenging to deal with, and the average babysitter isn't familiar with their diagnoses or their experiences. Before Respite Care, we kind of just didn't go places, or we didn't go out without them. Ethan has a hard time going out and being away from home, so we were pretty stuck in some ways. It's been really liberating to drop them off at KOTM and go out for the evening, even if it's a homework night for me with no kids, or we go to Costco, or we go on a date."

Respite Care is so much more than giving these parents a chance at a date, although that is important too. With respite services, we can, for a moment, shift the heavy weight of responsibility, concerns, worry, and physical load to someone else with the training and skills needed to care for their child. It's a huge relief. For just a few hours, the load is shared, and these parents are able to have a few minutes without the weight of the world on their shoulders. We come alongside these parents and, with this simple service, tell them, in a tangible way, "You are not alone; I can carry this for you for a moment in time."

THE IMPACT OF JOY

Yet the benefits of respite care do not start and end with the parents. We have seen every child who attends benefit as well. From social growth, an opportunity for autonomy, and just having the chance to be a kid and have fun, we see how much the program also means for each child.

Between delayed communication and a lack of age-appropriate social skills, many of our KOTM kids have few opportunities for unstructured play. For children with autism, a new environment can be overwhelming or overstimulating and cause them to shut down. A child who is scheduled for multiple therapies, such as speech, occupational, ABA, and so on, has limited free time for a parent to take them to a park or schedule a play date. But when they come to Respite Care, essentially for three hours, they can play or interact with other children as much or as little as they want. There is no pressure to perform or do anything they don't want to do.

Another benefit of Respite Care that is often unexpected is the way these kids are able to grow socially with each other and have a chance to experience a bit of autonomy, too. Many of these children have few opportunities to connect with peers, make friends, and socialize. Yet when it comes to our programs, the kids love coming and are excited to be in a place where they know they will have a great time. Because of that, many of them begin to use the social and communication skills they have been developing in therapy, or just enjoy time to play freely with other kids in a safe environment that is built for them.

Diane shared one such story, "We had one young child in our program for about two years, from age five to seven, and he barely made eye contact. We had a volunteer come many times, and he would hang out with him. Even though the boy would not interact, the volunteer thought, 'I'm OK with this; he knows I'm here. And he can just move around and do what makes him happy. He doesn't look at me or have me do anything; he can just know I'm here.'

Then, one night, the young boy turned to the volunteer, looked him straight in the eye, and said, 'OK.' The volunteer was just blown away; this was the first time in a year and a half the child had ever done anything like that. I see the children who come in nonverbal, and because of the socialization, paired with the therapy, school, and the work their parents do, they become verbal."

These kids, no matter the diagnosis or disability, have so much work to do in order to learn what comes easily to typical children. And they need every minute of therapy, school, and practice. But they also need fun; they also need a safe place where they can just be a kid, breathe freely, and have a chance to play with other kids. And for many of them, Respite Care is that place.

A KIDS ON THE MOVE MOMENT
Teri Houskeeper, KOTM Parent

Ryan was diagnosed with autism when he was eighteen months old. It was a gut punch. I was totally blindsided, honestly. My daughter Riley was just so ahead of the game when she was a baby; she knew all her letters, numbers, and colors. At eighteen months, she knew everything, and she just was on it and talking in full sentences. And so, when Ryan wasn't, I just thought, "Oh, he's just developing at a normal pace." Or, people say, boys develop a little bit slower, and so I didn't really think much of it. But at his eighteen-month well-check, it was clear to the doctor something was off, and we soon after got the official diagnosis.

Fast forward to today, Ryan is now thirteen and was recently also diagnosed with ADHD. And for the first time, we were trying to find the right medication for him. Our hope is that it would help him sit still so he could integrate more into the typical classrooms. With ADHD, you have to guinea pig your child to find the right one. Some meds will be successful, and some not, but you don't know until you try it. And for us, the process was horrible. Looking back, we call it the five months of hell because Ryan was manic; he didn't sleep for months and started self-harming even though he had never self-harmed before. It just was terrible. Ryan had a lot of outbursts and a lot of rage.

Ryan had been a sweet, adorable, kind, loving child; I had never wanted a break from him and was always content to be around him. But as we were trying to find the right medication and manage his symptoms, all of a sudden, I realized, oh, I do need some time.

Teri, Ryan, and Riley Houskeeper

I had never applied for state funding or looked for any sort of program—but now I needed it. So, I started doing research, but I couldn't find anything where we lived. It's ironic when you think about it: you can hire a teenage neighbor down the road to babysit for a home with five kids for $12. But to find someone that will take just one special needs individual, they charge $20 an hour for someone who's going to hide out in his bedroom the entire time.

So, when Diane called and said they had a spot available in Respite Care, we were thrilled. It would be free, and my husband and I would finally have the chance to do something just for the two of us.

The first two times we went, at pickup the staff told me that Ryan cried the entire visit. On the drive home, I just felt horrible and beat myself up. I kept thinking, "We're never coming back. This is horrible. We're never going to do this again. He was a burden. They hate him." I was so upset, and the whole car ride home, I was thinking the whole experience had been a failure.

That evening, I got a text from one of the Respite staff members saying, "Don't give up; we will find something that he enjoys." They went on to make suggestions of things they could try next time and asked my thoughts on activities he would enjoy. The next day, I got a phone call and an email, all encouraging me that just because it was a hard time doesn't mean it would always be hard. And they had all these suggestions, and I felt better about trying again. It was nice to know that he wasn't an inconvenience or a burden; the staff was prepared, they understood, and there was no judgment. And sure enough, the next time we went, he turned a corner.

Now, every time we get in the car, he asks if we are going to Respite Care because he loves it so much. Or if he knows we are going that night, he'll go and wait by the car, and I'll tell him that we're not leaving for three more hours and to come back inside. One time, I came to pick him up, he took one look at me, and he ran away! That never, never happens!

When your child can't communicate, it's hard to find someone that you trust with him. But sometimes you just have to hope for the best. You hope that if something happens, your child will tell you; you hope they have a good time. To find someone that you trust, who is affordable, competent, and reliable, is practically impossible. It's amazing to have this chance.

WHAT DO YOU NEED?

The demands of parenting a child with special needs can be overwhelming, and it's crucial to recognize that parents facing these challenges are not immune to the struggles and emotions that come with them.

One staggering statistic that often goes unspoken is the high rate of divorce among couples raising children with disabilities; surveys show it can be as high as 87 percent.[17] The pressure and stress can take a toll on even the strongest relationships. It's a testament to the immense challenges they face daily. Just because you're a parent of a child with a disability doesn't mean that you cease to be a human being with your own needs and desires.

Currently, we can only offer each family respite care one Friday or Saturday a month for three hours. This program operates solely on the generous donations of money from our supporters and the precious time given by our amazing volunteers. Our families appreciate this support, but we are acutely aware of the waitlist and the need for more.

Imagine if we had the resources to ask these families, "What do you need?" and could tailor a care program accordingly. It would be life-changing for these families if we could offer Respite Care to each family once a week. The burden on parents would be significantly lightened with consistent support they can count on. No more falling behind on errands, no more hoping for a rare evening out to enjoy an adult dining experience. What if we could support a family when they are experiencing hardship or are in crisis? For a season, we could offer Respite Care multiple times a week while they stabilize their family. The impact would be immeasurable.

---

17   Ann Gold Buscho, "Divorce and special needs children," Psychology Today, February 28, 2023, accessed November 8, 2023, https://www.psychologytoday.com/us/blog/a-better-divorce/202302/divorce-and-special-needs-children.

What would be possible if we created and designed a building with a dedicated space for Respite Care to support the families and children of all ages, and created safe spaces and activities for them to thrive in? What if their siblings could come along, simplifying care even further for parents and offering even more support? It sounds impossible, but as we have proven time and time again, impossible just means it hasn't been done yet.

YOUR MOVE
Become the First Layer of Respite Care

If you have a friend or family member with a child with a disability, I want to challenge you to be their first layer of respite care. Reach out and offer to care for their child, giving them a much-needed break to do whatever they need to do. I understand that what I'm asking may sound intimidating. You might need to learn how to communicate with the child or how best to care for them, but I can guarantee their parents will be more than willing to teach you.

You are allowed to have boundaries. You can specify how much time you can offer or discuss any aspects of the child's care you're uncomfortable with so you can work together to find a solution. You don't have to be their savior or their only form of support; the goal is to find what you can do to lighten their mental and emotional load.

This can be as simple as making space for them in the plans you're already making. Go out of your way to invite them to your events, your vacations, and your playdates. Many of these families are often excluded or simply choose not to go because the chosen playground to meet at does not have inclusive equipment. All you need to do is ask, "Is there a playground your child enjoys? Maybe we can meet there." You could even take a daily chore off their plate. Offering to pay for a house cleaner once a month would allow them to spend less time on chores and more time enjoying their family. Or maybe pay for a grocery delivery subscription for the year, saving them countless hours of time.

Being that first layer of respite care doesn't have to be scary or all-consuming. There is something that everyone can do to help, no matter how small, to make a significant difference in these families' lives. The challenges of raising children with disabilities are immense, but together, we can lighten the load for these incredible parents and their amazing children. It starts with a simple question: "What do you need?" Let's make a difference, one act of support and understanding at a time.

CHAPTER 7

INCLUSION IS FOR EVERYONE

*"There is no greater disability in society,
than the inability to see a person as more."*

—ROBERT M. HENSEL

If you were to read the story of Becca Winegar, academic career and prowess, you would never know she was born with Down syndrome. In high school, Becca, who is the daughter of KOTM co-founder Brenda Winegar, attended the neighborhood high school, participated in extra-curricular activities, and spent time with her friends on the weekend. Becca also discovered her love for music, recalling, "During my high school years, I was involved in the choir. I could express myself through music and realized music is a part of my calling." Clearly drawn to the performing arts, Becca focused her studies on drama and music.

After graduating high school, Becca began volunteering in the laundry center of the Provo Utah Temple and has done so for the last twenty-one years. She also continued to pursue her education in the performing arts at Utah Valley University. She would again find a dedicated group of professors and friends who saw Becca's talent and continued giving her opportunities to grow her gifts. Like any college student, Becca used those years to explore who she wanted to be in the world, explaining, "I was at the point in my life where I felt like I wanted to branch out. I wanted to find my inner self, find the things that I was good at, and I was able to do that from one of my very first professors."

During her collegiate career, Becca worked on dozens of shows, from performing in *Oklahoma* to directing iconic shows such as *It's a Wonderful Life,* and more. "I just flourished," Becca explained with a smile. "And it really helped me find myself and my voice through the art of directing. So many of my professors really helped to immerse me in this world, and I established good quality training in the directing and theatrical world. I could communicate my feelings through the power of the stage."

Unfortunately, Becca's amazing academic career and pursuit of the performing arts was not the typical experience for someone with Down syndrome when she was growing up. This was the mid-nineties, and while public schools often had special education programs, more often than not, those students were segregated into different classes and often in separate parts of the school campus from the typically developing students. This segregation was based on uneducated assumptions that children with disabilities would feel insecure if they couldn't accomplish what their typically developing peers can, and that their presence would slow the progress of the typically developing children.

Despite what was the norm experience and education track for students with Down syndrome, there were several luminaries in Becca's community who worked tirelessly to create more inclusive opportunities. At Becca's local high school, a teacher named Joe

Greer initiated a peer tutoring program, pairing typically developing students with those having disabilities, often individuals with Down syndrome. The integration of this program into the high school had a profound impact on Becca. Recounting the experience, she shared, "We would all pair off with each other, get to know each other, work together, and go into normal class settings. And during those years, I learned how to really talk to people and interact with people."

Becca Winegar

Just like any typical high school student, Becca's friendships have had a long-standing impact on her life; she shared, "I still hold those friendships dear in my heart because I know that my friends all love me. They embraced me."

Witness Becca's Remarkable Journey: From Brenda's Unwavering Faith to a Life Filled with Achievement, Independence, and Joy.

chasingtheimpossiblebook.com/chapter7

In the years since Becca completed her education, studies have revealed that learning spaces where typically developing children learn alongside children with disabilities enhance academic achievement and help *both* sets of children develop their social skills.[18] Additionally, a survey taken by the Special Olympics shows that the schools who participated in their inclusion program, Unified Champion, reported a 58 percent reduction in bullying.[19] They also saw that "both young people with and without intellectual disabilities who play sports together and socially interact develop life skills that benefit them long into the future."

We know now that inclusive learning opportunities and social opportunities are vital for the development of not just the skills and abilities of people with disabilities but for the social and emotional growth of the typically developing population, too. The work to create more inclusive opportunities is an endeavor that ultimately benefits everyone.

---

18   Silvia Molina Roldán, Jesús Marauri, Adriana Aubert, and Ramon Flecha, "How Inclusive Interactive Learning Environments Benefit Students Without Special Needs," *Frontiers in Psychology* 12, (2021): 661427, accessed December 13, 2023, https://www.ncbi.nlm.nih.gov/pmc/articles/PMC8116690/.

19   Special Olympics, "5 Benefits of inclusive education," Special Olympics, accessed December 13, 2023, https://www.specialolympics.org/stories/impact/5-benefits-of-inclusive-education.

A KIDS ON THE MOVE MOMENT

Michael Milius, Respite Volunteer since November 2020

Initially, I started volunteering because my wife needed credit for a class, just like every other student in her program. After she completed her credit hours, she had to direct her time elsewhere, but I just kept coming, and I'm still here. Interacting with the kids is definitely the best part.

There is this one family, they have three boys who are all in the Respite program, and every single time the parents come to pick them up, they want to get a picture with all of their volunteers from that night. As a supervisor it's something that I look forward to as I watch the parents come in and thank each volunteer who was with their boys that night.

Obviously, we emphasize how much volunteering means to us, but it helps keep things in perspective of how big of a deal Respite Care is for these families. Many of these student volunteers aren't able to return once they log their ten hours for the semester, so something as simple as the family wanting a picture to remember them really emphasizes what it means to these families.

Even if they only work with their child once, the family wants to remember them.

More than anything, volunteering at Respite Care has ultimately given me perspective. Before my time at KOTM, I haven't had much interaction with kids with disabilities. I don't have a sibling or friends with a disability, and I don't have kids who share some of their struggles. So, interacting with them at Respite Care has opened my eyes to how much effort and energy goes into caring for kids like this. My goal is to be a pediatrician one day, and I hope that these experiences will translate into how I care for kids in the future. Whether they have these disabilities or not, I see them as individuals and have insight and empathy into how much the parents are doing outside of the time that I'm interacting with them.

THE RIGHT TO TRY

Our founders, Karen and Brenda, intensely advocated for ensuring their children had access to the same activities and education as their typically developing peers and fostering those relationships. As educators, they understood that kids are more likely to try something new if they watch a peer try it first, and their children with Down syndrome were no exception. They also deeply understand the impact that an educator can have when they believe in the abilities of their students. Whether it's a peer or a trusted adult, children can only rise to the level of the bar set for them.

Kids, in general, want to be like their peers. Anyone with multiple kids knows that the younger ones typically develop skills faster than their older siblings did simply because they want to keep up. For example, when Reed was little, he struggled to learn how to tie his shoes, and Karen's attempts to teach him were getting them nowhere. So, what did she do? Karen recruited the neighborhood kids to help. She gave $5 to every kid in the neighborhood who helped Reed learn to tie his shoes. And you want to know how that turned out? Reed was tying his shoes by the end of the day.

When I was in high school, I wanted to participate in a school trip to New York City more than anything else in the world. Not only did my parents not have the finances to fund such a trip, they thought my dream was foolish, refused to offer me any assistance in fundraising, and took every chance they could to tell me that what I wanted to do was impossible.

As part of the fundraising program, I began selling pizzas door to door. I told myself, 'I don't care how many pizzas I have to sell; I am going to New York City.' It didn't matter what my family said or how they discouraged me, I was determined to fund the trip. So, without a car, the internet, or even the help of social media, I went door to door selling pizza orders, and when it came time, I delivered them door to door completely by myself.

And while the opportunity to expand my horizons and learn alongside my peers in the Big Apple was an amazing experience, I walked away with a bigger lesson that I learned from selling pizzas door to door: Anything I decide I want to do I can figure it out. In time, those small wins began to compound to big wins and my confidence increased. My belief in what was possible expanded and grew. I decided to start chasing the impossible.

When we simply have the opportunity to try something we have never done before, the lessons we learn along the way are incredibly formative. The impact of such lessons is not diminished when you have a disability, but oftentimes children with disabilities are denied the right to try.

When Becca and Reed were growing up, in the 1980s and 1990s, many educators held the same sentiment as Reed's doctor: when it came to someone with Down syndrome, you "shouldn't expect too much." As a result, many children with disabilities were denied access to learning alongside their typically developing peers as well as admission into extracurricular activities. Robbing them of the opportunities to try life-enriching experiences as well as the chance to develop those formative lessons that come with discovery.

It's also worth mentioning that Becca was not a child prodigy when it came to the performing arts. Like many of her typically developing peers in high school, before her first drama or choir class, she had never set foot on a stage. But we don't look at typically developing teenagers and deny them admission to a Drama 1 class their freshman year of high school. It certainly wasn't common for a theater program director to go out of their way to include and instruct students with Down syndrome. But a teacher took a chance, refused to assume that she couldn't learn, and gave Becca a chance. Not only did this prospect provide her the opportunity to pursue the arts as part of her future, but it endowed her with lessons that serve her every single day of her life. It built her confidence to try new experiences and explore new opportunities.

Today, we have clear examples of amazing people with Down syndrome living incredibly full lives and having varied careers. At the time we were writing this book, Mar Galcerán had been elected as Spain's first member of parliament with Down syndrome, Madeline Stuart is a professional model with Down syndrome who has walked New York fashion week, and Isabella Springmühl, from Guatemala, is a clothing designer taking the fashion world by storm, even after being denied to fashion school several times due to her Down syndrome diagnosis.

A Down syndrome diagnosis alone does not determine someone's abilities, even if they are in the same family. The year Brenda gave birth to Becca, her sister, Joan, also gave birth to a little boy with Down syndrome, Lindsay. When describing the effect the cousins had on the family, Brenda shared, "You can imagine the feelings, the heartache, and all that we went through. It was very difficult for our families. However, after recovering from the shock, both families came to a place of acceptance and went forward with these beautiful babies. Our families decided to do everything we could to make life as normal and healthy and happy as we could."

Luckily these sisters had each other as they tackled the many unknowns that come with raising a child with Down syndrome, and supported one another as Becca and Lindsay each grew and learned at their own pace. Brenda went on to explain the importance of believing in the kids and having expectations that, even though they are both unique, they can learn. Brenda encouraged anyone with a child with a disability to ask themself, "'What do you want for your child? What do you think you can expect, or what would you like to expect of them?' You have to expect if you're going to get any results. And it's everyday life. We live much better lives when we expect something to happen, but we must do something to make it happen."

Even if your child is different from another child with a similar diagnosis, their difference is not a hindrance, it's just unique. Brenda went on to explain, "The hard part to learn is that, [a child] might not turn out like this one or that one or that one, they probably won't. But things will turn out better than if they do not have the chance to try at all."

We have to give every child, no matter their abilities, the chance to hit the same bar as their peers. Empowering parents to educate their kids is absolutely foundational, but another piece of the puzzle is a community of peers, teachers, and friends who also believe in that child's ability to learn and grow. Every child is different, and whether a child hits that bar or not is not as important as allowing them to see how high they can rise.

INCLUSION IS A TWO-WAY STREET

When children with disabilities have the option to learn, play, and live alongside their typically developing peers, the benefits of inclusion go both ways. Whether it's in our childcare program onsite at KOTM or in their schools, when children are exposed to different types of abilities at a young age, they grow socially and emotionally. As a result, they become comfortable with different abilities and naturally develop a more inclusive mindset.

Simply from the nature of my work, whether it's a social event or we are volunteering as a family, my children have so many more opportunities to connect and play with children with disabilities. And it naturally has had an effect on how they see the world.

The impact of the exposure really hit me when my son was about five years old. He and I were spending the afternoon playing in a park near our house, and we took a break on a park bench. As we were sitting there, a runner with a prosthetic leg paused their run and grabbed a seat on the other end of our bench. His prosthetic leg is what is known as a running blade and had the eye-catching c curve and flashy steel coloring. When my son's eyes landed on the leg, they suddenly grew as big as saucers with excitement. He immediately made eye contact with the gentleman and enthusiastically asked, "Hey, where did you get that cool leg? That's the coolest leg ever!" Sure, he had many friends with prosthetics, but none as cool as this one. As far as he was concerned, this leg was straight out of *Star Wars*.

A shy smile crossed the gentleman's face as he responded to my son. "I had a special leg built for me." When my son sees people who are different, he sees possibilities, not limitations.

Inclusive programs and initiatives, like integrated classroom or volunteer programs, provide typically developing students and members of communities the beautiful gift of getting to know someone with a disability beyond their diagnosis. It's a chance to truly get to know and see someone. Making it possible to see someone like Becca not just as a person with Down syndrome, but also as an artist and someone like Reed as a community advocate. This, in turn, enriches our own lives.

As a culture, we are learning that no one person should be solely designed by one facet of who they are. Whether it's their socioeconomic status, race, job title, or diagnosis, we know that while these factors may influence someone's lived experiences, it does not define them. Yet, it is still too common for people with disabilities, particularly children, to be defined by their diagnosis or limitations.

Wayne, Jeana, Jaymi, Kaelyn, Bryn, and Alek Bonner

Jeana Bonner is an incredible mother to four wonderful children. Two of her children are typically developing and her other two girls, Jaymi and Kaelyn, have been diagnosed with disabilities: Jaymi with

Down syndrome and Kaelyn with Down syndrome and autism. Both girls' abilities vary greatly: Kaelyn is incredibly medically complex, requires assistance bathing, receives most of her nutrition from a bottle, and attends a specialty school that can accommodate her needs and provide her the opportunity to connect with peers her own age. Jaymi, on the other hand, attends her local high school, is learning to read, participates in cheer and is on the swim team, and is a very active teenager. While both girls are unique in their abilities, they both bring their own brand of magic to their communities and their schools.

Unfortunately, Jeana has had to fight almost every step of the way to ensure her girls have had the opportunities to learn alongside their peers, and be a part of their community. She recalled adamantly when we were discussing Jaymi's admission to the neighborhood school, "We felt like that's super important; they are just sponges soaking up what everyone's doing. So, we want her to be soaking up things from kids in a typical classroom. There's just a lot of research supporting that inclusion, and those environments are really key to that."

Jeana went on to explain that when Jaymi was in second grade, her special education teacher was supposed to bring Jaymi to the typically developing classroom several times a day, but was disheartened to learn this was not happening. "Every time we'd meet, we'd ask, 'Is she getting any time in the typical classroom?' And she would nonchalantly respond that oh, they hadn't gotten around to it."

Jeana continues, "One day, when dropping her off at school—she normally rode the bus—it just hit me that the kids with special needs got to school early. I know it's all busing safety, but they go to school early. They eat lunch alone. They had a recess alone with their group. They were in this classroom with just the other special needs classmates. They didn't mix with the [typical] kids. We had adopted her from a Russian orphanage and yet here we were, putting her back into the same system where she's just not integrating. Later, I would learn that the principal referred to her class as the 'district's kids,' not his kids. That's not OK with me!" Jeana ultimately decided to enroll Jaymi in a more inclusive school for the remainder of elementary school. But this was not the first time she would have to go to bat to ensure her kids had the opportunity to be included. And soon Jeana's fight for inclusion would grow to ensure her daughter's entire high school would not miss out on the benefits.

Jeana began, "A couple of years ago, our district was going to pull the kids [with disabilities] from Herriman and Bingham High School. There were only six kids with disabilities, including Jaymi, and they thought it would be better to bus them to schools that already had thirty other kids with special needs. They were trying to say that it's just not economically feasible to have a special ed teacher and aides for only six kids. But they don't see the increase in logistics when you have forty-five kids with significant disabilities at a high school; how are you going to integrate them into any elective classes? We fought them, but the teachers reached out to the parents and let us know they were not listening. And so, we had a petition signed by hundreds of thousands of people, and we went to the school board. They did make the policy change to transfer the students, but they were forced to reverse it."

Jeana went on to share that they were not just fighting for the six kids who have a right to attend school alongside their neighbors and the community, but also for the 3,000 other students in attendance at that high school. "If you just remove them, wipe them away, a large population never get the opportunity to be peer tutors, to go to games and interact with them, or to be part of Special Olympics."

Jeana continued to explain, "It changes everyone, and it changes your society. And if you're just going to wipe 'em away, it's like they don't exist, and they never get to go to school with their community. If they can go to school with their siblings and their friends and be seen instead of just being dropped off early and picked up late, it changes everyone's viewpoint and perspective. I sent both my typical kids to our district preschools because that's where their sister went. And I want them to be a peer model. I want them to see other kids with special needs, to know it's not just our family that knows how to interact with their sisters."

Today, their entire community benefits from Jeana's fight for inclusion. Jaymi recently participated in her first-ever swim meet. Jeana shared, "There are sixty kids at that swim meet, plus families and parents, and they're all just cheering their hearts out for her. Jaymi is a minute behind everyone else in the fifty freestyle, but she's doing it! It just brings something to the community, something I didn't really experience growing up. I know that my life would've been better had I had that opportunity to shift focus from what we think is important and see a different perspective in the world."

RECEIVING MORE THAN YOU GIVE

It is vital that we continue to advocate for the integration of communal spaces such as schools, parks, groceries stores, and more, ensuring they are accessible and welcoming for those with disabilities. It is also equally important that we normalize typically developing people actively connecting with people with disabilities, whether it's through a peer-to-peer program at school or through a volunteer opportunity like the ones we provide at KOTM. I cannot begin to explain how incredibly proud I am of our volunteer program. We literally have thousands of volunteers come through our door every year. Thanks to our close collaboration with the local medical school, many of them are medical students studying to become doctors and nurses. Others are retired and looking to fill time in their day, and others still are neighbors just looking to give back to their community. No matter the reason they come, by the time they leave, all of our volunteers are adamant that they received far more than they gave during the hours they spent in our building.

Most of them have had very little interaction or experience with children with disabilities. Our long-time respite volunteer Brittany Strobelt said it best when she explained the impact that volunteering has had on her, "You come to realize that we all just want to be loved and to find connection with other people. Volunteers will come because they have a class obligation or something, and they end up coming back, and some of them will bring friends. Yes, the kids are getting the connection, but the volunteers are too. It's so much fun to see where people are just having a good time on both ends. It's not just the kids, and it's not just the volunteers, it's everyone."

Another volunteer, Tadeo Peralta, found KOTM when his family participated in our Early Head Start program. He fell so in love with our mission that he soon volunteered. Tadeo shared, "I've been helping teachers in the classroom, and it's been a really good experience. I have even learned new ways I can care for my own child at home." Tadeo further explained, "In my home country, these spaces are typically seen as being only for women. It's been so nice because they're really inclusive and invite the men, the dads, to come and be involved in kids' education. It was the best."

At KOTM, we pride ourselves on setting a standard of excellence in our facility, our advocacy, and, of course, the support we offer parents, but one of the programs we are most proud of is our volunteer program. Yes, these amazing volunteers allow us to transform the lives of the families we serve, but we love seeing the transformation that happens inside of every volunteer. Each of our volunteers walks out of our doors into the community as better parents, more compassionate neighbors, and, in many cases, understanding and empathetic medical providers. The idea that our communities can be more inclusive is no longer a nice thought or an idea that a representative on the other side of the county is supposed to fight for. Instead, inclusion is something they can do every single day.

YOUR MOVE
Inclusion Is Easier Than You Think

As I have been interviewing the wonderful families who bravely volunteered to share their stories for this book, I have wrapped up each session with one final question, "If KOTM could wave a magic wand and give you anything you ask, what would it be?" And while the answers have ranged from funny to thoughtful and more, there is one that broke my heart.

When I asked Kendyl Madsen, whose daughter Monroe was born with fluid in her brain, this question, she didn't even blink before she immediately answered, "Don't park in the handicap parking."

With those clear-as-day blue signs and high fines, not to mention that it's just callous, it's hard to imagine that someone without a disability would park in a space designated for handicapped parking. Unfortunately, it happens all the time. Just the other day, I witnessed what appeared to be an able-bodied young couple pull into a handicapped spot. At first, I didn't think much of it, as there are different disabilities, and not all are recognizable to the eye. But as I passed by the front of their vehicle, I saw that they had no tag displayed on the windshield, and my heart sank.

Someone could need that spot.

There is a strong chance that when you take a spot, some mom with a child in a wheelchair now has to park further back. Hopefully, but not likely, there is a spot available for a ramp, and then navigate their child through a dangerous parking lot, both on the way in and out of the store.

Yes, leaving those spaces open for someone who truly needs them is important, but there is a bigger point that needs to be made:

Be more inclusive in the way you think.

According to the Pew Research Center, one in thirteen Americans has a physical or cognitive disability, and one in six children has been diagnosed with a disability.[20] So don't jump to conclusions or make assumptions about someone's abilities. Just because someone didn't need it at that moment doesn't mean that a family might not need it five minutes from now. Just because your child's friend isn't disabled doesn't mean they don't have a sibling who is. Just because you don't see the disability doesn't mean that there isn't one. These people are your neighbors, friends, and loved ones. They are worthy of your respect and consideration.

---

20   The Pew Research Center, "For disability pride month, 8 facts about Americans with disabilities," Pew Research Center, July 24, 2023, accessed December 30, 2023, https://www.pewresearch.org/short-reads/2023/07/24/8-facts-about-americans-with-disabilities/.

CHAPTER 8

NO SUCH THING AS IMPOSSIBLE

"Normal people run away from lions. They run as far and as fast as they possibly can. But lion chasers are wired differently."

—MARK BATTERSON,

IN A PIT WITH A LION ON A SNOWY DAY

Not one family we interviewed planned for a child with a disability, and I think that very few people do. From first-time parents, those who conceived with the help of IVF treatments, to someone like Brenda and Karen, believing they were done growing their family, and everyone in between, every family whom you have read about already had a plan in place. And when that plan went off the rails, each of these families was faced with the harsh reality of raising that child in a society that was not built with disabilities in mind.

Yet, every day, these parents face the daunting task in front of them and go to battle for their kids. They spend hours on the phone with insurance providers to get services covered, constantly shuffle their work schedules to make appointments, often pray they keep their jobs and advocate for their child at almost every single doctor visit and school visit. Then they go home and do their best to be present with their kids before they collapse into bed exhausted.

It sounds impossible, yet they make it happen every single day. They are driven by the love for their child to ensure they have their best chance at life; failure simply is not an option. And the same love and passion that drives these parents to chase down the impossible is what runs through our veins here at KOTM.

When our founders Karen and Brenda were hustling to find land for a building, they were told over and over again that it was impossible. Finally, one day, Karen refused to take no for an answer. She walked back to the hospital that had previously refused to help; she looked the board members straight in the eyes and told them, "You need us." From there, she explained how a unique partnership would not only allow the hospital to retain its non-profit status but help provide additional training for their doctors and nurses. To this day, the hospital is our good neighbor, and our current building still resides on that land.

Step into the Legacy of Karen and Brenda: Witness Their Journey from Parents to Trailblazers in Shaping a More Inclusive Future.

chasingtheimpossiblebook.com/kotm-founders

When I first came to KOTM, we annually raised around seventy thousand dollars in donations every year. At the time, the thought of raising one hundred thousand dollars seemed impossible. Yet today, we consistently raise *one million* dollars or more in donations every year.

At KOTM, tackling the impossible, defying the odds, and creating a path forward where there was none before is built into our very DNA. We know it's possible before there is funding, before there is a process, or before the resources are there. We have done it before, and we know we can do it again.

Along the way we have attracted and partnered with other people and organizations who are cut from the same cloth, like Diane McNeill, our Respite Care Director. When she founded the Respite Care program, Friday's Kids Respite, she had no money and no staff. Just a drive to answer the call of parents who desperately needed a break so they can continue caring for their children.

But why? Why would we continually go above and beyond to create these programs or offer these services when there are many other organizations that only offer a small portion of what we offer?

The answer is simple: parent power.

Our whole model is based on the premise that the parents are the best educators; the parents are our secret sauce. So, when we hear parents identify a gap in support, we start building bridges. As Karen has said from the very beginning, "We recognize that the therapist and support staff are vital. but it's ultimately their role to support the family. Teach the family; they are the ones invested in this child, and the family holds the key to helping. They will spend the time, spend the resources, and they'll be the cheerleaders all their lives."

This place was built with the belief that the parents are their children's best educators and advocates. As a parent of a child with a disability, Brenda said it best, "We've got to have the power if we're going to help our kids. If the parents have what they need, then the child will have what they need."

We understand that if we want children with disabilities to have a shot at a full life, we have to empower the parents and support the whole family. We're not just here to provide a service, check off a box and move on. No, we are doing what neither the government nor the medical system has been able to do: reimagining comprehensive care for children with disabilities that delivers results. It may sound impossible that a non-profit started by two moms out of their living room is accomplishing what billion-dollar organizations have not been able to figure out. But as you have read, we chase down the impossible every single day and have no plans to stop any time soon.

THE NEEDS ARE BIGGER, BUT WE'VE GOT BIG SOLUTIONS

During my three years as the CEO of KOTM, we have reached some big goals we set out for ourselves. As we celebrate our fortieth year serving the community, I am proud to say we have not let our foot off the gas. Currently, as a multi-million-dollar organization, we have doubled our operating capital, implemented a data tracking and analytics program to optimize systems, and increased our capacity to support over 3,100 children each year. While we are proud of these huge strides, as we have been deep in the planning process for the next growth phase here at KOTM, we quickly realized we were still not thinking big enough. Our recent conversations with parents have empowered us to identify the most consistent gaps in care that parents face and inspired an entirely new care model.

One of our parents, Teal Kalt, described, "In a perfect world, if there was a place where we could take Azure that had all of his therapists and services in one place, with people who understood his disability, and could also take his younger brother Rune, it would be my dream come true." As soon as I heard her desires, the faces and stories of all the parents I spoke with came to the forefront of my mind. They all shared this same challenge.

Ryan Erickson, the Chief Operating Officer of KOTM, was listening to the interview with Teal and had the same reaction as I did. We spent the next hour and a half redefining the needs of the families in our community, how we could bridge this gap in care, and give power back to the parents. If we filled in the gaps and provided the means to support the entire family, then each child would receive the best care, tailored to the entire family's needs.

There are three critical components that are vital to the care and development of every child with a disability: education, medical, and family support. We took a look at these three components and their supporting pieces to identify the following:

- How *should* education, medical, and family support ideally work together?
- What obstacles do families face when integrating all three components?
- How are these challenges being addressed currently?
- What improvement can be made in order to empower parents?

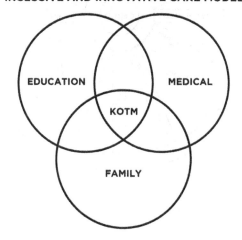

INCLUSIVE AND INNOVATIVE CARE MODEL

To explain further, I want you to think of a wagon wheel. At the center of the wagon wheel is the main hub; the child in the center and their parents are what's encasing them. Each spoke of the wagon wheel represents a different form of care that a child with a disability needs; each therapy is a spoke, education is a spoke, play and free time are a spoke, doctor visits and medical needs are a spoke, parent support and resources are a spoke, and so on. These spokes typically fall into one of those three main categories we described: a supportive educational space, medical care/access to treatment, and family support (such as respite care, sibling support, etc.). Now, picture the outside rim of the wagon wheel; it is the critical piece that not only binds the spokes together but also ensures the wheel can roll forward and make progress on the journey.

INDEPENDENT SERVICES

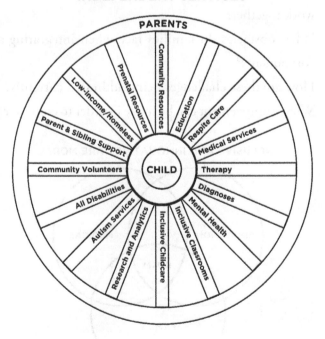

Currently, parents, in addition to the role they must play at the center of the wheel, supporting their child as a parent and caregiver, must also act as the outside rim of the wagon wheel; the critical piece that ensures everything works in harmony to ensure their child is progressing forward. Endlessly coordinating, scheduling, following up, and keeping the whole thing together to ensure their child is getting the care they need to move forward. This means they are required to be in two places at once, pulling double duty to ensure their child has what they need from them as a parent while also doing the heavy lifting of a care coordinator.

So, we began to ask, what if KOTM could fill that role of care coordinator? What if we were supporting the parents by bridging the gaps in care for them? What services are we missing in order to alleviate the pressure and burden on parents as they support their child? How can KOTM step in as the rim of the wagon wheel?

COMPREHENSIVE SERVICES

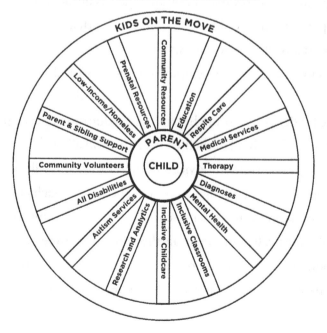

To answer these questions, we began meeting with more parents, medical specialists, leaders of similar non-profit organizations, and our state and local representatives. Between listening to the pain points of parents, the feedback experts, and, of course, a little courage to imagine the impossible, a vision began to appear.

This vision took shape as the Inclusive and Innovative Care Model. It's a revolutionary and comprehensive approach to care intentionally designed to provide education, medical care, and family support. An all-in-one facility where children can receive their education, access therapy, and receive some medical services, as well as family support services. In addition to this facility, each family will be partnered with a staff member who will serve as their care coordinator, working hand in glove with parents to design and implement an educational, medical, and support plan that works for their unique child and family needs. These Comprehensive Service Coordinators will continue to serve the family to oversee their services, assist in making changes when appropriate, and coordinate additional care as needed. Today, KOTM is unique, offering a golden standard of care that is unmatched and not found anywhere else nationally.

An integral part of developing the Inclusive and Innovative Care Model will be expanding our childcare and education program to include kindergarten through sixth-grade education or transportation to and from the school of their choice. This will allow families to keep their therapy and support services through KOTM. It will also provide us the opportunity to design a unique schedule for each child so they can receive therapy and attend school on the same campus. This will not only drastically cut down on the amount of time parents spend ping-ponging from one appointment to the next, but also empower many parents to keep their jobs. This revolutionary approach has the potential to overhaul the way our society supports families and children with disabilities.

INCLUSIVE AND INNOVATIVE CARE MODEL

EDUCATION

- Early Head Start Education
- Family Educators
- Inclusive Preschool
- Inclusive Childcare
- Parent Training and Education
- Floortime
- Great Beginnings
- Music and Movement
- Research and Analytics
- Kindergarten to Sixth Grade*
- Think Tank*

MEDICAL SERVICES

- Autism Clinic and Applied Behavior Analysis Therapy
- Medical Services Billable to Private Insurance
- Developmental Specialists
- Nurses & Psychologists
- Occupational Therapists, Physical Therapists, and Speech Therapists
- Mental Health Services
- Diagnoses
- Respite Care Services (6 Weeks to 18 Years)
- Expanded Days and Hours to Meet Parents' Needs for Respite Care*

FAMILY SUPPORT

- Community Volunteers
- Donation Center/Food Bank
- Parent Socialization
- Low-Income Families/ Homeless
- Sibling Support/Sibshops
- Prenatal Resources
- Inclusive Classrooms
- Community Resources and Support
- After-School Care*
- Community Gatherings*
- Wall of Hope*
- Comprehensive Services Coordinator*
- Transportation*

Future Center of Excellence and Expanded Services

As we currently do with our Preschool and Childcare program, typically developing siblings and members of the community would also be welcome to enroll their child in our school. This ensures every member of our community has the opportunity to benefit from an inclusive education. Typically developing siblings would also benefit from a built-in community that understands the unique gifts and challenges that come with having a brother or sister with a disability.

After school, children will have the chance to play and enjoy themselves, as children should, before being picked up. In the evening, we can continue to provide expanded respite care services and schedule therapies for parents to attend with their children after school.

This approach would free parents up to be exactly who they are supposed to be: not coordinators, air traffic controllers, or case managers, but their child's parent and biggest cheerleader. After leaving KOTM, they can take their kids home, cook them dinner, play a game together (with some hands-on therapy techniques thrown in, of course), and give lots of snuggles before resetting for the next day. These parents deserve what every parent deserves at the end of the day, the space to enjoy their family without the mental load and packed calendar that currently goes with managing their care.

If you are the parent of a child with a disability, you may be caring for your child for the rest of their life. There may be no eighteenth birthday or college graduation to mark the finish line of hands-on parenting. And while the support these families need does not lessen but evolves, the very least we can do is ensure comprehensive care in the years when development is directly connected to lifelong outcomes.

Yes, the need is big, but clearly, we are designing a massive solution that has the potential to revolutionize the approach to the care of children with disabilities. Just imagine the results if we all came together to advocate for and normalize comprehensive care like the Inclusive and Innovative Care Model. We would have more Reeds and Beccas sharing their gifts with the world. We would have kinder, more patient, more inclusive communities—the type of places we all dream of living in but struggle to find.

And this idea of building comprehensive services could spread to other communities in need because everyone can connect to some aspect of what we are doing.

LION CHASERS

In Mark Batterson's book, *In a Pit with a Lion on a Snowy Day*, he begins by calling out a little-known passage from the Bible. One that you may have only come across if, first, you are a Christian and, second, if you followed a one-year plan for reading the Bible. And even then, you probably would have passed right over it. The brief passage, located in chapter 23 of II Samuel, describes a warrior, Benaiah, who, one snowy day, despite the cold and slippery conditions, chased down a lion, followed it into a pit (or cave), and slayed the beast.

We've all seen videos or read headlines of people who keep exotic animals (such as lions) as pets. And, let's be honest, none of us is too shocked when we hear that these "pets" eventually turn on their owners. Instinctively, we know not to put ourselves in a situation where a dangerous animal could attack us. So, when I think of Benaiah, the warrior, confronting a wild, powerful, and probably terrified lion in a cave and going head-to-head...let's just say it takes guts to do something like that.

As Batterson continues to unpack the implications of this passage, he shares, "As I look back on my own life, I recognize this simple truth: The greatest opportunities were the scariest lions. Part of me has wanted to play it safe, but I've learned that taking no risks is the greatest risk of all."[21]

As I read the author's words, some of my greatest challenges, my lions if you will, began to flash before my mind: leaving an abusive home, rebuilding my life with no resources and no support, overhauling KOTM's approach to money and fundraising, and my current lion, raising $150 million for our new center and services expansion. Like Benaiah, I am a lion chaser; no one forced me to take on these massive challenges or big projects, but each time, I had a bigger vision than the one someone handed me, and I was not afraid to chase it down.

KOTM's last building expansion was in 1999, but we outgrew it in just a few years. This means that for over twenty years, we have been bursting at the seams and limited in the amount of support we can offer families and a community that desperately needs it. Until now, someone hasn't been willing to take on this massive project. But I am here now; I am not running away, and I'm ready to take this lion down.

Brenda and Karen had the same lion-chaser spirit. Raising a child with Down syndrome in the 1980s was no small task, let alone building a non-profit. At practically every turn, there was someone who had no problem letting these women know their disapproval. Once, when waiting in the grocery store checkout line with baby Becca, a woman tapped on Brenda's shoulder, nodded over to Becca, and said curtly, "I aborted one of those."

Despite the opposition, these women headed into the pit and faced down the skeptics, the "experts," the apathetic, and an entire system that denied opportunities to children with disabilities. They

---

21   Mark Batterson, "Excerpt from *In a Pit with a Lion on a Snowy Day*," Penguin Random House Canada, accessed December 30, 2023, https://www.penguinrandomhouse.ca/books/9577/in-a-pit-with-a-lion-on-a-snowy-day-by-mark-batterson/9781601429292/excerpt.

fought like lives depended on them because they did. When you head into a pit with a lion, victory is the only viable option.

Still today, I see time and time again that very few people are betting on these kids to win. But when their parents are empowered, they beat the odds every single time. And fifteen-year-old Brinley Bleyl is no exception. Born several weeks early, doctors performed CPR on her tiny premature body for fifteen minutes to save her life. However, due to the time her brain went without oxygen, she was diagnosed with cerebral palsy that affected her motor skills and brain damage that would affect her central nervous system. Doctors were not holding out much hope for Brinley.

Doctors did not expect Brinley to live long after being discharged; her father, Bill, shared, "It was not anything any parent wants to hear. I remember we went home from the hospital, and we kind of made the decision that we were going to enjoy every moment that we do have with her. We started to prepare for a funeral, and my mom was on her way out to help make plans. But the next day at the doctor's visit, they told us to hold off on preparations because she had hit some milestones. She was improving!"

Brinley Bleyl

Brinley's mother, Kat, went on to explain, "She's a fighter. She is a little spitfire, and it's amazing because we're sitting there, and we're the case with the worst prognosis. As we started her in therapy, I remember when one of the therapists came over to our house. He worked with her for a few minutes and said, 'It's not going to be good.' And I was so upset. I said, 'Don't count her out!'"

To say Brinley has beat the odds would be an understatement. Brinley has had more experiences in the first fifteen years of her life than many people have in a lifetime. She's been paragliding and water skiing, is an avid snow skier, and is out on the snow every week in the winter and more! As the family's adrenaline junkie, they know that if she has the chance to go fast, she is in! Bill went on, "She loves fast, she loves speed, she loves roller coasters. I mean, she loves anything like that!"

Just like Brinley, every single child and family that walks into our doors are lion chasers. And every staff member here at KOTM is ready to stand beside them as they head into the pit. So, if you were to ask us: *Why are you so hell-bent on creating a revolutionary program and taking on a massive construction project, isn't what you have good enough?*

The answer is no. Lion chasers refuse to live in fear of the lions hiding in the caves.

We're done telling parents to "hang in there" or "I'm so sorry, we wish we could do more. All we can do for now is put you on the waiting list until we have an opening." Those platitudes mean nothing when they collapse into bed exhausted every night and pray they can somehow find a way to make all the puzzle pieces fit. Every child we work with deserves more than a "let's see what happens" attitude. And every parent deserves access to the resources and support they need so that their children can, in turn, thrive. We know the needs, we know how to address them, and we are going to once again overcome the impossible.

But it's not enough for us at KOTM to be lion chasers alone; creating a center of excellence for children is a mantle that we are all called to carry. Whether you're a director of a similar organization, a volunteer at your child's school, or someone looking to find a way to give back, we are called to chase down these lions, not to accept the bare minimum and do what needs to be done.

"But Rachelle, I don't have a child with a disability; this isn't my fight."

It's simple to distance oneself from families facing disabilities. It's tempting to believe it's not your fight if certain checkboxes aren't ticked. Yet, just because you don't currently have a child with a disability doesn't guarantee the future. One day it could be your child, niece/nephew, or grandchild. When I first began working with KOTM, there was no one in my family or extended family living life with a disability. There is no way I could have foreseen that it would not always be the case.

During the process of writing this book, I watched my great niece Mica at six months old battle her first and second rounds of an aggressive central nervous system cancer called Atypical Teratoid Rhabdoid Tumor (ATRT). After two brain surgeries and two rounds of focal proton radiation this past year, her parents and sister are incredibly thankful she has survived. They are now starting to piece together what life will look like moving forward. Although she has survived these treatments, since the cancer persists, the uncertainty, developmental delays, and fight continue. Today, Mica lives with one paralyzed vocal chord; it's unclear if it will heal, and to ensure it prevents malnourishment, doctors placed a g-tube so she can receive nourishment directly into her stomach. As a side effect of the radiation and chemotherapy, she has permanent hearing damage and will need the assistance of hearing aids. And, as you can imagine, she is behind on her milestones partially due to lengthy hospital stays while receiving treatment.

Despite it all, Mica, Rebecca, and her husband, Fred, are still finding something positive. Rebecca shared with me, "Our positive is that she made it through the treatment because there are a lot of kids that unfortunately don't make it through the treatment. A lot of the time when we're connecting with families all over the world on social media, we see kids are dying from the treatment and not from the cancer. You have to soak in the good moments. Because those are what get you through the hard moments. You'll realize through this journey how much stronger of a person you are and how much that actually impacts other areas of your life as well."

Fred, Rebecca, Catalina, and Mica Saucedo

After Mica's most recent brain surgery, another complication arose: a fluid-filled mass formed on the side of her tiny eighteen-month-old head. Doctors could safely drain it, but it quickly filled back up. A flurry of tests and evaluations later, a new diagnosis and treatment plan were in place: hydrocephalus, and Mica will need to have a shunt surgically placed to drain the fluid from her head into her abdomen.

Nothing is guaranteed. After Mica's first surgery and round of proton radiation therapy, there were three beautiful months when she was cancer-free. As a family, they went to Disneyland and celebrated with a few other activities and parties while they began planning for the dynamics of rebuilding life after cancer. That is when they received the news that a new tumor had grown and they would need to restart treatment immediately. As you can imagine, the toll that constant treatment, in addition to the effect of central nervous system cancer, has on a toddler's body is a heavy one. We have all the hope in the world, but we also cherish each day that Mica is with us. Whether she is with us for another year or another one hundred years, she has already left a deep impact and legacy. As I look at my own children, I ask myself, "Was I as intentional today with them as I could have been? Did I truly make space to let them know how loved they are and how much joy each of them brings me? How can I show up more in the ways they need me?" Mica is a gentle reminder that you never know what lies ahead for the ones we love, and all we can do is to truly soak in the moment, fleeting as it may be.

Every time I think of the strength of my eighteen-month-old great niece, I'm in awe. Not only has she survived ongoing proton radiation therapy, two brain surgeries, and the placement of a g-tube, but she will now have a shunt placed, AND she still attends early intervention therapies, working hard to hit those milestones. The strength, resilience, determination, and fight within kids like Mica, Monroe, Ethan, and Kohen is humbling. If these little people with such little bodies can move mountains and do hard things, then so can we. As adults and members of the community, the very least we can do is match their determination, find our grit, and get to work expanding what inclusive care models and communities look like.

Rebecca shared, "I think that sometimes people fall into the trap of, 'I'm not a doctor or I'm not a scientist. I can't solve cancer. I can't cure cancer.' But what are the things you can do? I'm fine with doing paperwork, but having somebody that helps coordinate any of that headache would have been incredible, because it took so much time. And I'm also supposed to be working a full-time job on top of all of this. Just having somebody who's willing to do a little googling here and there for you is also something that's a little underrated. It goes a long way. Sometimes, support is as easy as just being willing to advocate. Advocate for things that maybe you don't have a personal connection to at that point. But you can care about people, and that can mean a lot in and of itself. Being willing to reach out to people who can make changes in laws and the programs available to people. Being willing to have another name on a list." We are all part of a community, and it's essential to recognize that a rising tide benefits everyone. If those most in need are taken care of, it creates ripples that spread to everyone.

The reverse is also true; when these families do not have support it also affects our entire community. Studies show that children with mental illness who do not receive needed treatment have a high likelihood of becoming violent toward their mothers and eventually other members of their community.[22] Studies also reveal that the more severe the disability, the greater effect it has on a mother's ability to work[23]

---

22 Darcy Ann Copeland and MarySue V. Heilemann, "Getting to "The Point:" The Experience of Mothers Getting Assistance for Their Violent, Mentally Ill, Adult Children," *Nursing Research* 57, no. 3 (2008): 136–143.

23 Michael Y. Wondemu, Pål Joranger, Åsmund Hermansen, and Idunn Brekke, "Impact of Child Disability on Parental Employment and Labour Income: A Quasi-experimental Study of Parents of Children with Disabilities in Norway," *BMC Public Health* 22, (2022): 1813, accessed December 21, 2023, https://bmcpublichealth.biomedcentral.com/articles/10.1186/s12889-022-14195-5#Sec6.

and their long-term earning potential.[24] And the long-term effects of not being able to make ends meet do not stop within the four walls of a family's home but impact an entire community.[25]

Across cultures, centuries, and religions, humanity's most revered and enduring leaders have all shared one thing in common, the call to stand in the gap and care for those who need help. Mahatma Gandhi once said, "The true measure of any society can be found in how it treats its most vulnerable members."

In the 25th chapter of Matthew in the King James version of the Bible, Jesus taught, "Then shall the righteous answer him, saying, Lord, when saw we thee an hungred, and fed thee? or thirsty, and gave thee drink? When saw we thee a stranger, and took thee in? or naked, and clothed thee? Or when saw we thee sick, or in prison, and came unto thee? And the King shall answer and say unto them, Verily I say unto you, Inasmuch as ye have done it unto one of the least of these my brethren, ye have done it unto me."

When we think about the most vulnerable in society, it truly is children, especially children with disabilities, as their needs are magnified. A child is so dependent on their caregivers, and their community, to feed them, clothe them, nurture them, teach them, protect them, and love them. It's a beautiful thing to know, that when we give of our time, talents, resources, and monetary donations, it's as if we are abundantly giving to Jesus Christ. We can know with a surety that we are giving in a way that He would also give.

---

24 Victoria DeFrancesco Soto, "What we lose when we lose women in the workforce," McKinsey, June 3, 2021, accessed December 21, 2023, https://www.mckinsey.com/featured-insights/sustainable-inclusive-growth/future-of-america/what-we-lose-when-we-lose-women-in-the-workforce.

25 Carina Mood and Jan O. Jonsson, "The Social Consequences of Poverty: An Empirical Test on Longitudinal Data," *Social Indicators Research* 127, (2016): 633–652, accessed December 21, 2023, https://www.ncbi.nlm.nih.gov/pmc/articles/PMC4863915/.

When we do nothing, these families become the silent sufferers of a society that places more value on productivity than the value of human life, AND the quality of that life. Ensuring these children and their parents have what it takes to live a life with dignity, respect, and love is the concern of an entire community.

Today, it's commonplace to find ways to separate ourselves one from another. We divide ourselves by political beliefs, religious affiliations, and especially when we decide not to help one another. Brenda and Karen could have made that choice. They could have said, "I'm sorry, but we have enough on our plate trying to help our children with Down syndrome; we cannot help a child with cerebral palsy, autism, or juvenile depression and anxiety." But they didn't. They instead found ways to grow, to serve and to meet the needs of everyone who walked through that door.

And we're not stopping now. Yes, we're tackling some of our communities' biggest challenges, but we refuse to leave anyone behind. Everyone gets to come. We are getting in the pit with a lion, and we're asking you to as well.

OUR MOVE

This book is by no means the period at the end of the KOTM story, but the beginning of a conversation. We would love to see more organizations and programs link arms, the same way KOTM has, to create centers that offer excellent, best-in-class services to members of the community who need it most. We want to teach others how to advocate and lobby at the state and federal levels for better funding, better protection, and more coverage from private insurance.

At KOTM, we understand that we are called to be trailblazers in these areas, but not everyone has that gift. Some people have to see it before they can believe it, and we want to be a resource to them as well. We would love to help anyone interested in replicating the gold standard of care we are developing. We will do our part to continue to develop and elevate what gold standard care looks like for these families and their children, but that work cannot stop with us. We need you to come alongside us if we are going to make moves.

First, if any part of our program would benefit your community, we would love for you to replicate it. Our team is here to pass along the systems, curricula, and programs that are working. We can even consult and offer assistance as you tailor it to fit your community's unique needs.

Second, we seek partners to help us achieve our vision here at KOTM in Utah. Developing our new center and trailblazing a new approach to care will take a lot of expertise, resources, and willpower. And if you have caught the vision for this revolutionary idea, we would love to have you alongside us.

If your heart is telling you to give, please give. Don't wait. Don't delay. Choose to take action and donate. May you receive an abundance and outpouring from the heavens as you generously give. One father in our Respite Care program shared, "If I had a potential donor in front of me, I'd probably cry. You have the potential to change somebody's life, whether it's the parents who need a break or whether it's the child who needs to go to a judgment-free zone where they can feel accepted, play and be loved for who they are. That's what you can offer someone. It really makes a difference for that one family, that one person." His wife added, "And when you make a difference for one person, it doesn't stop there. That changes society as a whole in its own time, in its own way. There's just no end to the good that will keep coming from helping families."

**MAKE YOUR MOVE: DONATE TODAY
TO TRANSFORM TOMORROW!**

KOTM.ORG/DONATE

Whatever your level of involvement, each of us needs to do our part to chase down these lions and to make a move. Creating stronger communities, a kinder society, and a more inclusive culture is something we all need because, at the end of the day, a rising tide lifts all boats.

ABOUT THE AUTHOR

Rachelle Rutherford is the Chief Executive Officer of Kids on the Move, a multimillion-dollar non-profit serving children with delays and disabilities. Rachelle is passionate about the most vulnerable members of society, namely children. She holds a dual title as Mrs. World America and Mrs. World America Fitness 2023–24 with "Defend Innocence" as her platform—protecting children from all forms of abuse. Rachelle has been a member of the Board of Directors for Prevent Child Abuse Utah for more than a decade. She has a lifelong love for education, earning dual undergraduate degrees in Business Management and Finance and a master's degree in Business Administration. Rachelle is a speaker, business consultant, mentor, and co-host of the *Purpose Powered* Podcast. She is the owner of Elevated Capital Consulting and Elevated Executive. Rachelle has an entrepreneurial spirit and has spent over twenty years in executive leadership roles within many diverse industries: commercial real estate, education, genealogy, information technology, and telecommunications. She leverages her leadership experience in business, applying her knowledge and expertise using data analytics. Rachelle loves a good challenge. She is gifted in her ability to drive revenue and profitability, taking companies to the next level. Rachelle lives in Lindon, Utah, with her husband Scott. They have six wonderful children: Grant, Evan, Grace, Eva, Aubri, and Gabe.

CONTACT

Website: rachellerutherford.com

Kids on the Move: www.kotm.org

Instagram: @rachelle.rutherford

TikTok: @rachellerutherford

LinkedIn: Rachelle Rutherford

Purpose Powered Podcast: PPowered.com

**MAKE YOUR MOVE: DONATE TODAY
TO TRANSFORM TOMORROW!**

KOTM.ORG/DONATE